HALIFAX 1842

Catherine Howe

◆

HALIFAX 1842
A Year of Crisis

for those like
Patience Kershaw and Benjamin Rushton

Foreword by Stephen Roberts

BREVIARY STUFF PUBLICATIONS
2014

First published by Breviary Stuff Publications

BCM Breviary Stuff, London WC1N 3XX

www.breviarystuff.org.uk

Copyright © Catherine Howe, 2014

Foreword © Stephen Roberts, 2014

The centipede device copyright © Breviary Stuff Publications

Cover design Paul Mangan

A CIP record for this book is available from
The British Library

ISBN: 978-0-9570005-8-2

Contents

Acknowledgements

I give heartfelt thanks to Stephen Roberts for his kindness in making critical comment and for giving advice and encouragement during the writing of this book, and to Ian Winstanley for making available his essential research into mining history. Also my thanks to Paul Mangan at Breviary Stuff for his patience, and for publishing and making available this book to everyone who might be interested. And thanks to all at the Halifax Reference Library, especially Anne Jackson and Natalie Midgley who gave unstinting help and showed great patience during research periods. Also those at the Calderdale Archives Services at Halifax, Bradford, Leeds and Wakefield and, not at all least, my thanks to the historians who have contributed their work to the Halifax Antiquarian Society's Journals, past and present.

Foreword

This book tells a story that deserves to be more widely known. It is a story that is not found in the text books that are used in schools. It is a story that cannot be discovered in the general histories of Victorian Britain that are to be found in bookshops or public libraries. It is not even a story that, in the town where it occurred, is known to everyone who lives there. It is the story of a working class community that fought back against the ruling elite that inflicted on it low wages, unemployment and near-starvation. It is the story of how working people united to demand a say in the law-making of the country. It is the story of Halifax in the West Riding in summer 1842.

In Halifax in the second quarter of the nineteenth century thousands of hand workers toiled all week for a wage of five shillings and subsisted on oatcakes and potatoes. The weavers were left idle when their employers did not put out yarn, and were fined for spoilt work. These impoverished, put-upon men were aggrieved by the introduction of power – in 1827 James Akroyd had built his first power loom shed. Their leader Ben Rushton, who looms large in this book, spoke of the weavers being 'annihilated'. The plight of the combers was no better. Many of these worked in their own dwellings, where their charcoal-fired comb pots increased temperatures to almost unbearable levels and gave off harmful fumes. Already, in 1825, they had taken part in a long strike. There were also a number of small mines on the outskirts of Halifax, where women and children dragged loads of coal for up to a mile down narrow passages. One of these was seventeen-year old Patience Kershaw. Her description of her days of intolerable labour from 5am until 5pm, working alongside naked men, shocked those who read it. Catherine Howe – herself a songwriter – first became aware of Patience Kershaw through the song 'The Testimony of Patience Kershaw', performed by the north east folk group the Unthanks. She writes with considerable sympathy for Patience Kershaw and with considerable respect for Ben Rushton, weaver, one-time Methodist preacher and most popular of speakers in chapels and at open-air camp meetings.

It is little wonder that Halifax became a stronghold of support for the anti-Poor Law agitation that grew from the attempt, in 1834, to abolish outdoor relief for the poor, for the ten hours campaign and, ultimately, for Chartism. They saw men like Akroyd ("The greatest tyrant in the town") as their enemy and the Chartist leader Feargus O'Connor, who was often amongst them, as their saviour. The People's Charter, published in 1838, demanded, in its famous six points, the participation in law-making of all men. By December 1838 the working people of Halifax were marching to the first of many West Riding demonstrations at Peep Green in the Spen Valley. When the Bradford publican 'Fat Peter' Bussey left for the Chartist Convention in London in February 1839, he took with him from the West Riding 52,800 signatures for the National Petition, 13,036 of them from Halifax. For over a decade Halifax was to remain a bastion of Chartist support.

This book discusses the early years of the Chartist struggle in Halifax, including the rising-that-never-was in winter 1839-40. What comes through in these early chapters about the clandestine meetings and nightly drilling is the determination, resilience and militancy of the local movement. At the heart of the book, however, lies a narrative of the dramatic events of August 1842 which culminated, on 16 August, in an attack on a military convoy taking prisoners to the railway station at Elland. Dorothy Thompson has observed that in this year more force was thrown against the authorities than in any other year in the nineteenth century. Across the industrial districts of England great turn-outs of working people took place in response to wage cuts imposed by employers. Mills were shut down as working men flooded them by drawing the plugs from the boilers of the steam engines. Ben Rushton, at a huge meeting at Skircoat Moor, denounced the masters for reducing wages and called for peaceful support of the strike and for the People's Charter. Defiantly, as soldiers were deployed to contain them, the people sang Chartist hymns. Serious trouble was brewing. When the cavalry cleared the streets with their sabres, a violent response became inevitable. A civil engineer was detained by his own men: 'We two are to watch thee, like', he was informed. 'Thou'rt not to be fettled but thou 'art to be kept inside o' t'house'. On Salterhebble hill the convoy carrying the prisoners was attacked by a hail of stones and bricks, and several soldiers were wounded. These extraordinary events are told graphically and powerfully by Catherine Howe. For those who want to know the detail of what happened on that momentous day, this must now be the definitive account.

Ben Rushton was arrested in 1842, but not brought to trial. Known – according to inclination – as an 'old bald headed rascal' or 'the beloved veteran in the people's cause', Rushton was to speak at the great meeting that took place on Skircoat Moor on Good Friday 1848. His funeral, in June 1853, was to be the last great Chartist demonstration in the West Riding. Thousands arrived by special trains, or walked over the hills. Rushton died a poor man, but was widely-loved and deserves to be remembered in this book.

When asked what she does, Catherine Howe does not reply 'historian' but 'songwriter'. She is something else as well: a Halifax lass through-and-through. This book has not been written by someone who considers herself an expert on Victorian social history. She has not immersed herself in the debates amongst scholars about what Chartism was or was not. Frankly she's not interested in all that stuff. What she is interested in is recovering the stories of working people with whom she clearly identifies. I like the way she writes in such obvious sympathy with these people, the way that she juxtaposes great events with the smaller events of individual lives, and the freshness of many of her judgements. This is an important story told with real empathy. I hope you enjoy it.

Stephen Roberts
Visiting Research Fellow in Victorian History
Newman University
Birmingham

Preface

Halifax is where I grew up. My family came from the south of England, so I am first generation Yorkshire. When I was a child our garden gate opened on to Skircoat Moor where tens of thousands of Chartists rallied during the 1830s and 1840s, and there I played, without any knowledge of the Moor's history but always with a sense of it. One of my earliest memories is hearing, surprisingly because by then it was rare, the sound of sheep when one of the last of the outlying farmers brought his herd down the Moor and on, into Halifax town. My brothers, sisters and I could hear the noise of their bleating and then their beating hooves before we saw them, ghostly little bodies, as if they knew and were trying to tell us that, after generations, there were but a handful of years before they would come that way no more, would never been seen again. For me, this was history in the making, or perhaps in its passing, and in this way, I think, the history of Halifax flowed in my blood before any understanding of it. It is important to hear the voices which once spoke in your street. I am hardly surprised to find that there, right on the doorstep of my childhood home, so many voices were raised for a better life. I was lucky enough to have been brought up in its midst, even if it did happen more than a hundred years before I was born.

After completing an Open University Degree Course in 2000 which inspired my interest in social change, I began to write. Being a songwriter by trade, it is apt that it is a song which started this most recent research into Patience Kershaw and her home town of Halifax in 1842. Frank Higgins wrote *The Testimony of Patience Kershaw*, which was nominated for inclusion in the Best Original Song category of BBC Radio 2's Folk Awards in 2010. It has been made famous by Sally Rogers and by the English folk group The Unthanks, and I am so glad that they and Frank Higgins introduced me to Patience. Patience is one of the millions in England who, one hundred and seventy years ago, lived and worked in conditions which, many said, were beyond even the experiences of those who fell victim to the West Indian slave trade. The lives of British workers were described, by some, as 'White Slavery'. It was an emotive phrase which spoke true. In this book, Patience stands for all the children and young people, all the working people, the mine workers and factory 'hands', of these times.

My purpose in writing this book is to tell the story of the disturbances at Halifax in August 1842; there is no presumption to add to the analyses of these events. Any mistakes or unorthodox views contained here are mine alone.

Catherine Howe

Beginnings

1
Mines and Mills

Once, the hills overlooking Halifax were covered with coal mines, 'there is scarce a hill but you find, on the highest part of it, a spring of water, and a coal-pit'.[1] Patience Kershaw lived on one of these hillsides and worked down one of its pits, at Boothtown in Northowram township, which lies within the large parish of Halifax, Yorkshire. In physical terms, Boothtown lies on the eastern slope of the small Lee Brook valley which runs down to Halifax town from the north. In 1842, Patience was sixteen or seventeen years old. Her birth date is not entirely clear; even she was unsure of it. She seems never to have been christened, and the same can be said of all her siblings. In fact, it is likely that her parents were never officially married but this possibility did not keep them from having a large family together. Patience was born in 1826, give or take a year, to Elizabeth. Her father, John Kershaw, was a coal miner and, by 1842, Patience could very easily have been working for ten years at one of the coal mines close to the terraced cottage where she and her family lived on Plough Croft Lane. All of Patience's nine siblings did mining work at some time in their lives. It tended to be a family enterprise.

The coal mine Patience worked down was Boothtown Colliery, and on Saturday, 15th May 1841, she was approached there by a stranger called Samuel Scriven. Samuel Scriven was a young man of thirty-three years who had been sent from London to look into the employment of children in the northern mining districts. This was, partly, in reaction to a terrible event that had occurred three years earlier in Yorkshire. On 4th July 1838, eleven girls and fifteen boys, some as young as eight years, were found drowned together after a thunder storm sent massive amounts of water down into the pit tunnels at Clarke's Colliery, in Silkstone, Barnsley, where they worked.[2]

Reports of this disaster appeared in leading newspapers and, until this kind of attention made it impossible, it was known by next to no-one that children worked down coal mines, not even by those living in the towns where it happened. This and a long-fought campaign to reduce the working hours in textile mills brought a team of sub-commissioners, appointed from a London office, to the North country to look into child employment and Samuel Scriven, one of the sub-commissioners, made his way to Yorkshire as soon as he received his instructions, first to Leeds and then Bradford. Once at Bradford he decided that, for his purposes, he must take up his position, 'in the most central locality [and] I hastened to Halifax, via Keighley and Denholme'. On leaving Denholme, he happened to see his first mine workers as they walked along the road. They turned out to be, 'a little gang of hurriers returning to their homes. Many of them were very young and amongst them one of five years of age. They had come to their work that morning at six o'clock and stated that they generally left at six at night, sometimes later'.[3]

Samuel Scriven arrived at Halifax at the very end of April, 1841, and set to work on the first day of May by inspecting Bins Bottom Colliery mined under the southern slopes of Southowram hillside. He went on to see two more pits before the end of that day and he quickly discovered that his task would not be easy. He was met with suspicion by the miners who did not welcome any interruption to their work and to their way of doing it. They seemed uneasy at the exposure of the state of their children working beside them. The following Thursday, 6th May, he descended into Quarry House Pit in Northowram, owned by Joseph Stocks, one of the three major land and pits owners in Halifax. As he arrived at the pit bottom, an extremely large stone just missed his head as it fell after him from the unlined shaft.

The Stocks, Lister and Rawson families were the three dominant mining employers in the Halifax area. They seemed to hold a more sanguine attitude to child labour than their miners. The younger Joseph Rawson, speaking of Halifax's Swan Bank and Bank Bottom mines, which his family owned, told Samuel that he did not know how many men they employed, or how many children. He answered Samuel's questions like this:

> All the children are hired by the colliers and are paid by the week, I
> believe, but I do not know much about that... It is the practice of both

parties to go into work together and come up together. I do not know whether they get their breakfasts before they go [or] get any at all. They do not get any dinners in the pits. They get nothing until they come out again when they have done their work, sometimes at four o'clock, sometimes at seven.[4]

Likewise, George Emmet, proprietor of Wells Colliery at Norwood Green, had no idea how many children he employed, he had no idea when they came to work and left, and whether or not they ate during the day. There were no girls down his mine. Miners stripped-off to work and the propinquity of naked men and boys to part naked girls he thought 'indecent and immoral'. Mr. Emmet did not feel himself responsible for anything that might happen to the boys while working at his mine.[5]

Samuel Scriven continued to inspect the mines at Halifax, Low Moor and at Huddersfield for another two weeks before arriving at Patience's Boothtown Colliery, owned by Joseph Stocks. Boothtown Colliery was, in fact, a day hole. Day holes, or tail end mines, were tunnels at the base of a hill and, generally, they required no winding machinery for bringing workers to the surface.[6] Even if Boothtown Colliery did not need this machinery, it was still mined extensively. Its tunnels ran as far as two thousands yards, and Samuel Scriven entered them as he had entered many others in the past two weeks. One of the miners, a man called Samuel Wells, explained to him that the seams of coal were, in the lower bed of coal, from sixteen to eighteen inches, in the upper from twenty-two to twenty-four inches high. Ponies could not be used to haul the coal, so children did the job.[7]

Samuel Scriven and Patience Kershaw met on Saturday 15th May. He saw that she, like all the rest, was filthy and ragged. She is, he lamented, a 'deplorable-looking object, and such an one as the uncivilized natives of the prairies would be shocked to look upon'. Patience was dressed in trousers and jacket, both in a terrible state.

"I go to pit at 5 o'clock in the morning" she told him. "I hurry the corves a mile and more". This means, Patience was working at least twelve hours each day pushing or pulling a wagon, called a corve, full of coal just hewn by her miner from the coal face to the main gate where it was emptied, then back again for more. There was no pause in this work; the miners generally got the coal faster than the hurriers transported it. Sometimes the children were left to finish off the day's loads alone. This was a hurrier's work.

Patience also had a bald patch on her head. "The bald patch upon my head is made by thrusting the corves," she explained to Samuel Scriven. The corves were made of wood, they were heavy and ran on small iron wheels. When loaded they weighed between two to five hundredweight (100 to 250 kilograms) and they required head and arms to push. She and her fellow hurriers pulled and pushed the corves through a mile or more of extremely low and narrowly mined tunnels at Boothtown Colliery which were sometimes a little more, sometimes a little less than three feet high. Each round trip, from coal face to the main gate, took about one hour for they had time for some eleven journeys each day. Because the work involved huge and constant physical exertion, Patience had muscular legs, arms and shoulders. "My legs have never swelled" she said, but her sister Alice's had "from hurrying in cold water when she was hot".

> [T]he getters that I work for are naked except their caps; they pull off all
> their clothes; I see them at work when I go up; sometimes they beat me,
> if I am not quick enough, with their hands; they strike me upon my
> back.[8]

Working at her mine, there were, she said, about twenty boys and fifteen men. She was the only girl. "The boys take liberties with me sometimes, they pull me about; I would rather work in mill than in coal-pit".

The local mines, which entrances peppered the high hillside above Boothtown, were generally not of the deepest. It is said they were sunk to a maximum depth of some fifty yards and never below the level of the valley bottom because of drainage. Some workings were only a dozen yards or so below the surface and once the coal had been hewn and brought to the surface, packhorses took it down the hillside from the pit-heads into Halifax town.[9] Although a shallow pit, there still is the possibility that trappers were used at Boothtown Colliery. Patience may well have started her working life in this way.

Trappers were infants; five, six or seven year old children, who sat in the tunnels in a hewn-out space beside wooden ventilation trap-doors which were critical to safety. Without ventilation, gases, 'fire-damp', could accumulate and explode. Each trapper held a string which was attached to the trap-door. As soon as an approaching corve was heard, the infant would pull the string to raise the door. The corve and hurrier would pass by, and then the infant would let the door fall back into place. The only light the infant ever saw during its working day was the candle burning on the corve as it rolled by on its journey to and from the coal face. As the hurrier and corve disappeared down the tunnel, total darkness and solitude enveloped it again. Infant trapper and child hurrier would do their work for at least twelve hours each day, for which they received a handful of shillings at the end of the week. There was no water to drink. Patience's weekly wage was paid by the miner she laboured for because the mine owners preferred not to know that children, girls especially, worked down their mines. This is how it was for the mining children. Quite wonderful is how Samuel Scriven sometimes found that their dispositions were cheerful.

Above ground, and half-a-mile or so down the Lee Brook valley from Boothtown Colliery, owners of the great Halifax textile mills employed many more children in their 'many-windowed-mills' than the mine owners on the hillsides.[10] At least the mill children, more visible than those in the mines, were supposed to have some protection from uncontrolled industrial usage through an Act imposed in 1833. Now, under the 1833 Factory Act a child cotton mill worker who had yet to reach his or her thirteenth birthday could legally work only nine hours a day, those aged from thirteen to eighteen, twelve hours a day. Everyone older than eighteen was free to work as long as they wanted.[11]

This legislation applied only to cotton mill workers. The Halifax worsted and woollen mill owners had succeeded in keeping their businesses beyond the terms of this law and too many cotton mill manufacturers bound by it found ways round it, making the small provisions of the 1833 Factory

Act ineffectual. In the Parish of Halifax, 'the Master Manufacturers are dead to every feeling but of *interest* –

> the cursed "lust for gold" has so engrossed their minds, and absorbed their whole hearts, that they view their work people as part of those inanimate machines by which is their pride and boast, even the infant portion of their slaves shares not their protection and regard!'[12]

Magistrates in industrial towns were 'mitigating, even nullifying, legal penalties' when judging breaches of the 1833 Act, because many of them were mill-owners themselves and, in some cases, were sitting in judgement on their own family businesses.[13] 'I say that in the worst sense of the word these magistrates are thieves and perjured men', wrote Richard Oastler who, in 1830, had initiated the campaign for a ten hour working day for mill workers.[14] Nor was it good that, under the 1833 Act, every child must pay sixpence for a surgeon's certificate of age. It was calculated that, by 1838, the state had received some £12,000 through this charge; almost three-times that of income from fines extracted from manufacturers violating the Act, which stood at £4,422.[15]

Halifax surgeon, James Holroyd, who had rooms at Number 9, Cheapside, and whom Samuel Scriven would come to know quite well during his stay, came to realize three years after the Factory Act had been passed, that the employment of children in the Halifax mills was, in reality, an entirely unregulated and barely acknowledged practice. Children flitted from one employer to another while many of their parents had not the faintest idea where they worked. James Holroyd knew many of the Halifax mill owners, and he approached them with the idea that they should form a system whereby a child employee must produce a note of discharge from its previous employer before another might take it on. This attempt at local regulation seems a good idea although its main purpose was to improve the morals of the children. 'It is … in their moral condition that these persons suffer the most' he said.[16]

Concerns over these young operatives' moral condition did not necessarily imply a sense of care towards them. These children were not viewed as innocents to be cherished and nurtured. In the middle-class religious minds of the day the tendency was to view children as original sinners to be saved, and only the saved could properly fill their place in society. These children happened to be industrial workers and, as long as every industrial worker, old and young, could read the Bible and would go to church, the moral system through which they would learn to be socially valuable and trustworthy workers would be upheld. By this was their moral condition defined. Because of this some mill owners supported a modicum of education for their workers to do away with 'vice and ignorance' and to improve the standard of their workforce.

The physical dangers to which a mill child was exposed 'on account of the dangerous state of the machinery from the want of proper boxing off', was a secondary consideration and injury was generally regarded, even by the concerned James Holroyd, as due to 'want of care on the part of the children'.[17] Halifax's textile mill children might not, at first, have welcomed Holroyd's regulatory system as it restricted their ability to escape with any kind of speed a cruel overseer; a manoeuvre they fairly often needed to employ. But James Holroyd was not necessarily to know this, at least not until Samuel Scriven made his report which shows how imperative this tactic was to many of Halifax's child-hurriers, who were beyond even the illusory protection of the 1833 Factory Act.

2

Halifax and Its Workhouse (1837)

Halifax, although so far up from sea level, is surrounded by hills. Northowram to the north, Southowram to the east, Warley hillside to the west. Only to the south does the land fall away from the town, down a road called Salterhebble Hill to a 'sweet' and narrow valley where the canal runs 'sharpish westwards' towards Sowerby, the river Calder southwards, on to Elland which lies between Halifax and its neighbouring town of Huddersfield seven or so miles off.[18] These hillsides are still green and covered with trees, cut through by dry stone walls set in the time of Patience's grandfathers on what had been open hillside.

The hills surrounding the town presented a problem to Halifax commerce because they made transportation of goods difficult. North and Southowram hillsides had been cleaved apart by the great Godley Cutting in 1830 in an attempt to ease the transport problem by road. Halifax's nearest railway line was the Manchester to Leeds which, in 1842, had only recently opened and did not come through Halifax. Travellers had to get off at Sowerby Bridge or at Elland and take an omnibus from there into Halifax town.[19] Bradford's nearest railway station was at Brighouse. So transport into and out of Halifax was a commercial difficulty to mill-owning and mine-owning families.

There were, of course, the canals but until the system was extended into the town, Halifax's manufacturers had to get their produce down the hill to Salterhebble Docks. One who was enamoured of the canal system is quoted as enthusiastically claiming, '[o]ne horse will pull as much weight on the Calder and Hebble Canal as a string of six hundred pack-horses can carry'.[20] One canal horse could certainly pull the weight carried by one hundred packhorses, which is impressive enough. Packhorses were still being used as late as the 1850s for the local transportation of wool and cloths, and for the carrying of coal from the North and Southowram pits down into the town.

At Plough Croft Lane there runs a geological fault which throws the coal deposits up to an outcrop seam which stretches, southwards, towards Range Bank.[21] As well as coal, there were clay pits. And these Northowram hillsides were also managed by eighty or ninety farmers.[22] The terraced cottage in which Patience's family lived, along with all structures in the area, is built of stone and roofed with slate. Almost certainly, the rows of cottages still standing on Plough Croft Lane contain the one in which Patience and her family lived in 1842.

Patience lived there with her mother, Elizabeth, and eight of her ten siblings, Hannah, William and Sarah, Bethel and Alice, James, Solomon and Caroline. Her father, John, had died in 1839, eighteen months before Samuel Scriven's arrival at Halifax, and now the family was headed by their forty-six-year-old mother. The most senior brother, Thomas, was married and living separately but not far away. And Patience's oldest sister, Sybil, also was married and living down the valley, under the shade of the Crossley family's Dean Clough mill. Sybil was a factory worker and very likely working at the expanding Dean Clough carpet mill or, possibly, the Akroyd family's great mill at Haley Hill from where materials were exported around the world.

When Patience met Samuel Scriven she faithfully listed the names of every member of her family to him. She thought her brother Thomas was thirty years old. Thomas was more probably twenty-six in 1841 and, like his father, was a miner, a getter, at the coal face. His younger brother William also was a miner. Another brother, Bethel, of similar age to Patience, was a hurrier along with the boys James and Solomon. Sarah and Hannah had been hurriers but had switched to mill work as weavers. Alice, aged fourteen or fifteen, was sick and at home, so spending time with her infant sister Caroline and their mother. The family members still living on Plough Croft Lane brought in between them, from their work, about £2.10.00 a week. A good income for a working family.

Many of their neighbours were silk weavers or woollen combers and earning considerably less per household. The Scholfields lived a few doors down, and next-door to them James and Hannah Greaves with their five children, also a much younger Harry Clayton with his wife Jane and three infants, all three were silk weaving households who must have been taking work from Thomas Atkinson's silk spinning mill lower down the hill at Boothtown. And in the cottages along this high hillside row lived Abraham Nicol, a shoemaker, with his wife Harriet and six children. Robert Stott, a labourer, and his wife, recently married, were the Kershaw's immediate neighbours. There was one other mining household, and another headed by an engineer. Also living close to the Kershaws up Plough Croft Lane were two blacksmiths, and the fields through which the lane ascends were farmed by Jonathan Wood.[23]

Plough Croft Lane runs, unceremoniously, straight up the sharp ascent from Boothtown at some 325 metres above sea level to the old Bradford Road. Halifax Town lies at around 140 metres above sea level. So in 1842, when Patience left her terraced cottage shortly before five o'clock each morning to go to her work at Boothtown Colliery, just a few moments' walk downhill, she had a bird's eye view of Halifax town. In the early light of the summer months she might briefly cast her sight over the smoking chimneys of the cotton and woollen mills and of the dwellings of rich and poor, way below her in the valley, before she descended into the underground for the next twelve hours or so, to hurry the corves. Halifax, from Patience's view point, was not an unbeautiful sight.

Although mining had been going on across the hillsides of Northowram township for some two hundred and fifty years — shafts sunk then abandoned and filled, others newly sunk, leases granted and profits made by leaseholders and landowners — Halifax was mainly a cloth town. Cotton, wool and worsted was spun and woven there, still in some combers' and weavers' cottages but more and more often within the new system of factories, especially in the case of spinning because spinning was already successfully mechanised. The expansion into factory working, even in Patience's short lifetime, had been meteoric.

Now in the immediate Halifax district there were about forty-nine cotton mills, twenty-one worsted mills, thirteen woollen and one silk mill, as well as nine others producing mixed fibres.[24] And steam power was more and more used. Coal produced the steam and was the only source of power beyond muscle, water and wind, and it conquered all before it. Patience's muscle-work in the tunnels of Boothtown Colliery was critical to national prosperity and her generation was the one to shoulder the worst effects of the huge social changes taking place.

In reaction to these changes, so welcome to the industrialists, so unwelcome to skilled manual workers, sprang up workers' Radical Associations in the industrial areas. Halifax parish was unusual in having as many as ten.[25] One of these Radical Associations met in the township of Ovenden, another in Queenshead, on the road to Bradford.[26]

Over at Ovenden, at Friendly Fold, clearly visible to anyone standing beside Patience's cottage and looking across the Lee Brook valley, lived a handloom weaver called Benjamin Rushton in a cottage standing behind a row facing the road to Illingworth, a mile or so to the north. Both communities were busy places. Benjamin Rushton had lived at Ovenden for most of his life and, in 1842, was a man of fifty-seven years, his wife Mary was a year younger and not well. She was suffering from advanced dropsy, or oedema, which can result from pregnancy and from malnutrition. Her body would be swollen and painful.

The importance of the religious life at this time cannot be overestimated and Benjamin Rushton was a religious man. He had spoken as a witness to his Christian Methodist beliefs for years as a preacher and continued to do so but his political convictions were not to be subsumed by Methodist dogma. He was prudent but he was not meek. Benjamin Rushton was a bold declaimer of working people's constitutional rights. He had headed local protests against the Manchester killings at St. Peters Fields in 1819 and, by the early 1830s, had offended his Methodist New Connexion peers because of his political views. Local working people had long respected him as a man who spoke up for their democratic rights and they now thought of him as, '[o]ld Benjamin Rushton, the Halifax veteran and one of whom Yorkshire has ever reason to be proud'.[27] At the end of his life a demonstration of no less than real love for him would be made by thousands at Halifax, and he remains a revered figure to this day.

Also at Ovenden lived eighteen-year-old John Snowden, a clever teenager but hampered by bad sight and who, like so many others, could not read or write. John Snowden did learn both skills as he grew older, and he, too, would receive unbounded respect from local people for his efforts to gain a better life for working men and women. Men of Benjamin Rushton's and John Snowden's stamp joined whichever campaign was locally available which sought to improve the lives of working people because, no matter how hard and for how long a person worked, hunger and poverty were the results. Working people badly needed political representation, having none.

In England and Wales in 1842, less than eight percent of the entire population had the vote. Eight percent of the population, to use a leading Chartist's expression, were 'all powerful oppressors', over the remaining ninety-two percent of men, women and children, and this small percentage was entirely male and predominantly aristocratic landholders.[28] Not one woman had the vote. It was constantly pointed out by radical reformers of the time that this fortunate eight percent lived in great comfort on the backs of the remaining ninety-two percent; workers like Benjamin Rushton, John Snowden and Patience Kershaw, who laboured in unregulated industries and often appalling conditions for the meagerest pay.

In Yorkshire factories, there were times when limbs were torn, fingers crushed, children beaten and inhumanely overworked; fines were imposed for late arrival at work and for damaged or imperfect items, wages cut for loss of work through accident and injury, and surgeons' bills to treat those injuries not willingly met.[29] In the land-owners' mines adults and children were regularly injured or killed from collapses, explosions and failures of apparatus, and there was no sense of owner responsibility for safety. Something had to give.

Britain, then, was a country where the vast majority of people lived and laboured under the inadequately responsible control of industrial and political masters. And one event in particular roused the working population of Britain and brought about the Chartist agitations of these years. This was the New Poor Law of 1834. The Poor Law had been in place since Elizabethan times and represented a tradition by which, in principle, the rich would ensure the poor did not die of starvation in times of distress. The New Poor Law of 1834 originated in a belief that, because costs were growing out of control, relief payments must be encouraging idleness amongst the poor.

To the horror and anger of the working people directly affected by the New Poor Law and also by many better protected who thought it a disgrace, it was decided that direct financial help to the chronic poor must end. Now the only help to those in need would be given inside the workhouse. All the small workhouses which had been dotted amongst the communities were closed and one large institution for each area was built in their place. The overall running of this system came from the London office of the Board of Governors. Centralisation had begun. And just to make matters worse was the policy that a workhouse should be as unpleasant a place as could be devised so that there would not be the faintest chance that any who entered would be glad to be there. They were not to be places of sanctuary. They were to be a deterrent to anyone thinking of seeking help. They were to be closer to places of punishment.

All workhouse paupers were given a job of work to do but never of the kind to undermine the value of work carried on outside the workhouse, so it was generally the same kind of work given to prison inmates, something in the nature of rock breaking for road building, oakum picking, which involved pulling apart disused hemp ropes for recycling, or crushing bones for fertilizer. But the greater grievance was that man and wife were separated and child separated from parent. The decades old practice of putting unprotected children out to work in the mines or the mills as apprentices continued. The term apprentice was too often used as a polite term for dispensable slave.

Richard Oastler, living as Thomas Thornhill's steward at Fixby Hall which overlooked the wheat fields and green pastures about Huddersfield, a man admired locally and known nationally for his campaign against 'Factory Slavery', wrote of the 1834 New Poor Law that, if he has the misfortune to be reduced to poverty, 'the man who dares to tear from me the wife whom God has joined to me, shall, if I have it in my power, receive his death at my hands!'.

> If I am ever confined in one of those hellish Poor Law Bastiles, and my wife be torn from me, because I am poor, I will, if it be possible, burn the whole pile down to the ground...[30]

This was horribly close to self-prophecy because Richard Oastler would have the misfortune to experience something very similar, very soon. In his case, for debt.

Some time elapsed after 1834 before the New Poor Law was imposed at Halifax. A representative of the London Board of Governors arrived there in the first week of January 1837 and elections for the selection of local Guardians for the workhouse took place in the following month. The job of the local Guardians was to see the new project through, then to maintain its running. They would not be popular men. £10,000 was borrowed from the government, a site was chosen and the building rose up on an open field between Gibbet Street and Hanson Lane, where Lightowler Road now runs. In all, the construction cost £12,000.[31] This fine, south-facing building of Yorkshire stone, which held four hundred beds, was opened for business on 25th March 1840. It represented a new order and it was feared, therefore hated, by the people of Halifax. They threw stones at it. It was called, by just about everyone, a Bastille. This is what Benjamin Rushton and Richard Oastler called it. Allusions to the French Revolution were not entirely overstated, as events would soon show.

3

The Beginning of the Chartist Campaign (1838)

The arrival of the New Poor Law to the West Riding of Yorkshire in 1837 really fired a national protest movement. Many householders and prominent individuals asked the Earl of Harewood, Lord Lieutenant of Yorkshire at the time, to call a county meeting to demonstrate against the new law. They failed to bring the Earl to action, so they acted alone.

On Whit Tuesday, 16th May 1837, not long after the workhouse Guardians were elected and had had their inaugural meeting at the Trustees' Office in a building on Cheapside, the roads leading from the towns of Halifax, Bradford, Huddersfield and all the outlying townships and villages around about, under beautiful, clear skies, were thronged with, at the very least, one-hundred-thousand people, all heading for Peep Green on Hartshead Moor to demonstrate their opposition to the hated new law. The effort involved in the organisation of this day, and in the attending of it, undertaken by working men, women and children on this holiday, was immense.

Imagine Peep Green, a great expanse of open land, on this exceptionally fine, cloudless morning, its dips and rises rapidly filling with thousands of people who, carrying flags and banners, had walked miles from every direction, accompanied by musical bands. The speakers' hustings were, 'built in the strongest manner, and better adapted for the purpose of public meetings than those we generally witness', wrote the reporter for the *Sheffield Independent*.[32] On the platform, ready to address the great assembly, were Joseph Crabtree from Barnsley, James Bronterre O'Brien, J.R. Stephens Methodist preacher, Richard Oastler, and Oldham's MP John Fielden. Not just these, but Feargus O'Connor, Henry Hetherington and Robert Owen, were there in support. The majority of these men were to be leaders in the Chartist movement and many had, or soon would, serve terms of imprisonment for their commitment to the improvement of working people's lives.

Most of the banners displayed Biblical inscriptions. 'The more these cruel tyrants bind us, the more united they will find us'; 'What God hath joined together, let no man put asunder', referring to workhouse separation of families, and 'Go now ye rich men, weep and howl for your miseries that shall come upon you'. The village of Meltham's banner simply read 'No Bastiles [*sic*] – England this day expects every man to do his duty, by showing his determinate opposition to the accursed Poor-Law Amendment Act'. By four that afternoon a resolution had been proposed and approved to petition the House of Commons through John Fielden.[33]

This great open-air meeting was a spectacular, well organised and optimistic event attended by a number of England's greatest social reformers, of that or any time since, and by more than one-hundred-thousand local people. It was one of many events to be held in the next few years, none of which made the slightest dint on the policies of government which was to keep the established way of things just as it was. Nevertheless, in this way, through the coming together of these people, the speakers, the families from the towns and villages, the members of the Radical Associations, and through their determination to change things, a petition known as the People's Charter of 1839 came to be.

The Chartist objective was to get a parliamentary vote for every man over twenty-one years of age, by which, they calculated, the governing elites would be made accountable to those they ruled. Feargus O'Connor, who was at Peep Green on that Whit Tuesday, became the leading inspiration of the Chartist movement. In Halifax Benjamin Rushton, John Snowden and Christopher Shackleton, all three from Ovenden, Jonathan Bairstow at Queenshead, young Benjamin Wilson and his older Skircoat Green neighbours Robert Wilkinson, Bill Cockroft and William Thornton and many others including Isaac Clisset, Robert Sutcliffe, Thomas Cliffe and John Culpan, all would be prominent in the local Chartist movement and would give much of their time to its cause. At Huddersfield, Lawrence Pitkeighly, a Scotsman who had come to live in Yorkshire some fifteen years earlier, was committed to social reform through the Charter, likewise his colleagues William Rider and William Vevers. Bradford's Chartist group was led by Peter Bussey. All were committed to political change through the demonstration of numbers and some, up to a certain point, were willing insurrectionists.

Feargus O'Connor was a red-head Irish barrister, not shy to use his fists whenever it became necessary. He could floor his opponents "like nine-pins," he said, and there were witnesses to the fact.[34] He was, perhaps, a man of great feeling and action before being a man of great reflection. He was new to Yorkshire. Having come from Cork to take up a seat in the House of Commons in 1833 (which he then lost in 1835) he travelled up to Oldham to secure support as a parliamentary candidate there. It was then that he saw how things stood with the people of the industrialised north. 'I saw England for the first time with the naked eye', he wrote, 'the pallied face, the emaciated frame, and the twisted limbs, wending their way to the earthly hell'.[35] One of his first, if not his very first visit to Halifax was in 1836 when he was invited to a dinner hosted by two of the town's leading local politicians, Charles Wood and Edward Protheroe, but when Charles Wood realized his guest was hostile to the New Poor Law, he and his supporters withdrew from the event. It was left to the Radical politician, Edward Protheroe, to welcome Feargus O'Connor to Halifax.[36]

After the great anti-Poor Law meeting at Peep Green in 1837 funds were raised so that six months later, in November, O'Connor was able to produce the first edition of a newspaper which he called the *Northern Star*. The *Northern Star* was printed at Leeds in the office of publisher and journalist, Joshua Hobson. It was a hugely important paper. It broadcast news of the Chartist movement. It gave coherence to the Chartist aim, not just in Yorkshire and Lancashire but nationally. And it was an instant success:

> The *Northern Star* made its first appearance, in the political horizon, amid the howlings of the wintry blast ... It is eight weeks since the "*Star*" took its position in the hemisphere ... There is not a Democratic paper in England, sold at the same price, whose circulation now equals

that of the *Northern Star*.[37]

In no time the *Northern Star* was selling, nationally, an astonishing 20,000 copies a week. And many more than 20,000 people would benefit from its pages, which were read out loud in beerhouses and private rooms and copies borrowed and shared. A network was in the making and it needed a national organisation to head it. The Radical Associations had lacked, 'unity of aim and method', said John Bates, a Queensbury man who had worked as a mine's gin-horse driver when a boy in the 1820s. 'When the "People's Charter" was drawn up …', he recalled, 'we felt we had a real bond of union, and so transformed our Radical Associations into local Chartist centres'.[38] These were remarkably optimistic times.

One of the first Chartist meetings at Halifax was called for Monday 22nd January 1838, at the Talbot Inn, at Woolshops. Snow had been falling but this did not stop well over three thousand people turning up. Imagine, suddenly, here was the promise of a national organisation dedicated to the political emancipation of the working people. Everyone who came to this Halifax meeting was cheered by two bands of music. It was held at the Talbot's Assembly Room, where its chairman, William Thorburn, began by saying it was not right that out of all the many thousands of people living in Halifax parish, only a few hundred had the vote. Parliament must be petitioned, he said, so 'the people of England were put in possession of the same privileges'. There were loud cheers.

So popular was this idea that the crush of people who arrived to hear it was too great for the Talbot's Assembly Room to hold. It was decided that everyone inside must move out to join the majority there. And so they did, and the rest of the meeting took place in the large area behind the premises where it was very cold and wet. Hand-loom weaver Robert Sutcliffe proposed a complete cure of their grievances through radical means. Then Benjamin Rushton came forward to speak.

He was used to speech-making. Under the falling rain, he stood, bald and bearded, and told the crowd that until they had the vote the aristocracy would continue to rob them. Taxation without representation was plunder. 'Hear hear,' they all replied. 'Universal suffrage is the object we have in view ...'. By universal suffrage Benjamin Rushton meant all men over twenty-one to have the vote.

> '[A]nd the aristocracy know it, yes they know it well, that with universal suffrage their fishes and loaves will dwindle into nothing, and it needs not logic to prove that they think only how they shall secure the enjoyments of life for themselves, and patient and obedient starvation for the people. How many of you are there that can earn only five shillings a week out of which you have to pay taxes, rent, food, fire, light, clothes and education![39]

A simple message, and true. John Crossland, also a loom-weaver, moved that a petition, embodying the meeting's resolution, be adopted and presented to the government. Thomas Cliffe told everyone he had little faith in the success of a petition, that if it is read at all by members of parliament it will just be thrown under the table, but that it is, nonetheless, a thing they must do, so he seconded it. And so a petition was approved by the Halifax Chartist group. Finally the three thousand who had gathered on that cold and wet day, made their ways home.

It was now, in April 1838, that one of the many events which were fundamental to the crises of these years took place; one of the thousands of events which, more often than not, were not reported and for which no land owner or mine proprietor took the slightest responsibility. In April James Lumley, a child of nine years, was killed in a Halifax mine through a fire damp explosion.

In the wider and more visible world, the terms of the Charter were written in London and published, on 8th May, under the title, 'The People's Charter'. Its main thrust always was that all men over twenty-one must have the right to vote for the laws under which they and their families were expected to live. People signed up to it in their hundreds of thousands. In fact many more than a million. Ten days after the publication of the terms of the People's Charter, Thomas Thornhill dismissed Richard Oastler, his steward for eighteen years, whose tireless public opposition to the new Poor Law system had become an irritant to him. Ominously, Richard Oastler by this time had run up heavy debts in the name of the Thornhill estate.

At Northowram, on 5th July, and unreported, happened the death of John Crossley, aged sixteen years, killed in one of the mines there when a scale from a corve hitting the ledges of the shaft as it was raised, fell on him. On 31st August, eleven year old Francis Taylor was killed through a fire-damp explosion. Two months later, Thomas Oldfield, a man of forty-eight years, was killed at Northowram when he fell down the mine's shaft.

Before the lower and more easily navigated turnpike road from Halifax to Bradford via Queenshead was laid, the way to Bradford had come up over Range Bank. This old road passes by the top end of Plough Croft Lane at Pule Nick, some 350 metres above sea-level, then on, over Swales Moor, through Catherine Slack and the township of Clayton before descending through bright, fine views of fields and small valleys, into the streets of Bradford.

In the years dealt with here, these hills between Halifax and Bradford were populated with hardy people, many farmers, weavers and combers and a goodly proportion of miners. One view of the old mining communities was that they were 'Infamous for knavery and cruelty, and the deplorable ignorance and rudeness of these savage villagers are not to be equalled in the Empire'

> There are fewer individuals in the [Clayton] township able to read and write than in any other place of equal size in England, and consequently the subjects which form topics of discourse and engage the minds of working men in other places are here never either discussed or understood, and whenever a number of the inhabitants are met together at an inn, obscene songs, the most disgusting conversation, brawling and fighting alone prevail ...[40]

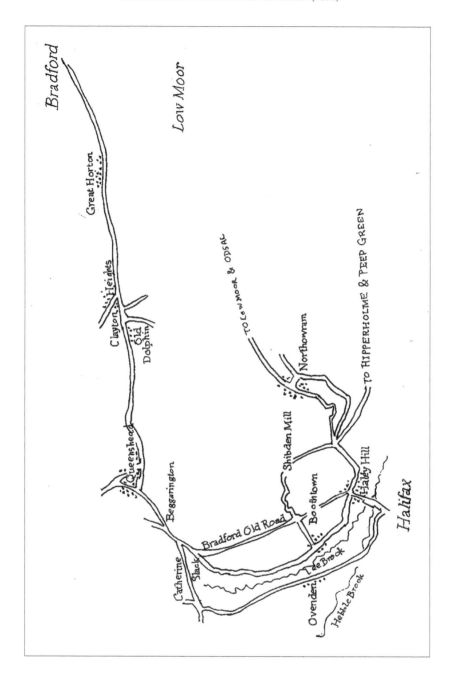

This is not a universally accurate view of those who lived on the hills between Halifax and Bradford, although polite society might then have thought so as, by 1842, it was recognised as an area of particularly strong Chartist feeling. The Bradford and Halifax Radical-cum-Chartists would sometimes meet at Queenshead to read papers and discuss current issues, and once the terms of The People's Charter were published, their main concern was to get signatures. In the final months of 1838 and the early part of the following year, many men and women from Clayton and Queenshead, Boothtown and Ovenden, went to Chartist meetings. This was replicated across Yorkshire and across the whole country. They met in huge numbers in fields, on moor tops and in towns to sign the petition and to elect delegates to represent them at a soon to be formed national Chartist Convention. Chartist lecturers tirelessly went about the country spreading the word. These were days of great hopes and massively expended energies. 'It is almost impossible to imagine the excitement caused by these manifestations' said one.

> The people did not go singly to the place of meeting, but met in a body at a starting point, from when, at a given time, they issued in huge numbers, forming into procession, traversing the principal streets, making the heavens echo with the thunder of their cheers ...[41]

As the days grew shorter, torchlight processions unnerved the government. The 'red light of the glaring torches, presented a scene of awful grandeur. The death's heads represented on some of them grinned like ghostly spectres ... the uncouth appearance of thousands of artisans who had not time from leaving the factory to go home and attend to the ordinary duties of cleanliness, and whose faces were therefore begrimed with sweat and dirt, added to the strange aspect of the scene. The processions were frequently of immense length, sometimes containing as many as fifty thousand people'.[42] For the most part, the politicians at London and the magistrates in the towns, at this time, just watched on in the first months of 1839. Some arrests were made of prominent and outspoken Chartist lecturers. J.R. Stephens, who had stood on the hustings at Peep Green in 1837, was one. 'Stephens ... openly preaches from his pulpit the necessity of the people being armed to prepare for the worst', wrote one of his colleagues.[43] After the arrest, Benjamin Rushton spent many weeks lecturing as far away as Skipton in defence of Stephens and raising funds for his defence.

People were assured the Charter would revolutionize their lives and that this liberation was at hand. With impressive swiftness, the Chartist message caught on. At a Radical meeting held at Halifax early in January 1839, Thomas Cliffe said he 'welcomed the improvement in trade – and especially the gun trade'.[44] And at Bradford, Peter Bussey held meetings of his Radical Association at his beerhouse. Bussey was a big man, physically and vocally. Some called him corpulent; all regarded him as a committed social radical. 'His countenance is indicative of much thoughtfulness, albeit there is an expression of restlessness and of stern resolve that cannot be mistaken',[45] said one observer. Within the coming year, this impression of stern resolve would be revised by all who knew him.

On Monday, 13th January 1839, Peter Bussey was guest of honour at a dinner held at the Odd Fellows' Hall at Bradford where the Bradford Northern Radical Union's green silk flag displayed the words 'Free we will live, or free we will die'. And inscribed across a banner fixed below the platform where the speakers sat:

> On with your green banners rearing,
> Go grasp every sword to the hilt;
> On our side is virtue and Erin,
> On theirs is the parson and guilt.

Then, two days later, he made his way up the hill from Bradford to Queenshead to another dinner, held at the Half Way House Inn. Lawrence Pitkeighly came from Huddersfield and introduced the mixed gathering to his companion George Julian Harney, a young Kentish man, grey eyed and ruddy complexioned, born into a seafarer's family and now living in Sheffield, one of the movement's leaders who had come to inspire the people of Halifax, Huddersfield and Bradford with the Chartist message. Harney's belief, in unequivocal language, was, 'Let there be no blinking the question ... the fact is that there is but one mode of obtaining the Charter, and that is by INSURRECTION'.[46] Despite its revolutionary overtones, this was a polite evening's gathering at Queenshead on that winter's night. A toast to 'The People' was made, then one to 'The

Ladies'.[47] Other meetings would be less decorous and less open to scrutiny. In South Wales, Chartist activity would become intense. Here, by the end of the year, a planned uprising was to come to something.

4

The Nature of the Chartist Campaign (1839)

A branch of the Anti-Corn Law League was formed at Halifax in February, 1839. Ever since 1815, the Corn Laws had allowed duty to be applied to imported corn if home produced did not reach a set price. This artificially kept up the price of home-grown crops and boosted the profits of landowners (who at this time held roughly two-thirds of the seats in the House of Commons). The Anti-Corn Law League was composed of middle class men, mill owners and mine owners, who objected to the Corn Laws because they saw it as legislation imposed by the landed aristocracy to advance their own interests. The 1830s is the decade in which these middle class men tasted political power for the first time and they wanted more. One of the League's tactics was to argue that the Corn Laws made the cost of living too high in a time of trade decline and which, they quite reasonably added, was crippling working families.

But there was more to it than this. The impoverished working families were, in fact, the industrialists' home market. The industrialists wanted their workers to have enough cash to buy goods beyond food. And they wanted this without having to pay them more. By their reckoning, repeal of the Corn Laws was the way to achieve this, not better wages. The Anti-Corn Law Leaguers bought their labour at the lowest possible price because it made economic sense to them. This did not seem cruel or immoral to the majority of them because, by now, the law of economy was a science. The making of money was barely subject to any moral sense as it once had been.

One Chartist leader, Ernest Jones, echoed the moral teachings from the twelfth and thirteenth centuries when he stood before a crowd at Halifax and said, 'A man must work before a grain is grown, or a yard is woven ... as labour creates all wealth, labour is the first thing bought – 'Buy cheap Buy cheap!' ... But now comes the next: 'Sell dear! Sell dear!' Sell what? *Labour's produce*. To whom? ... to the *labourer* himself! 'Buy cheap, sell dear.' How do you like it? ...

> Buy the working man's labour cheaply, and sell back to that very working man the produce of his own labour dear! ... The employer buys the labour cheap – he sells, and on the sale he must make a profit; he sells to the working man himself – and thus every bargain between employer and employed is a deliberate cheat on the part of the employer.'[48]

This is how the Chartists saw the matter.

Halifax industrialist Jonathan Akroyd presided over his local Anti-Corn Law League branch, and fellow mill owners John Holdsworth and Francis Crossley held membership. It is worth noting that in this month while the middle class Anti-Corn Law League convened its branch at Halifax, the Chartist National Convention, representing the working classes, met for the first time, on Monday 4th February, at the British Coffee House on Cockspur Street in London. This is a moment when future opposing ranks simultaneously formed; when battle lines were drawn. Working class distrust of the property-owning middle-classes had been raw since the 1832 Reform Act when working people, thinking themselves allied to the middle classes during that particular fight for democratic rights, had been left in exactly the same position after legislation was passed. They were left powerless, to face punishing conditions imposed by their supposed allies.

In 1839, at the first meeting of the Chartist Convention at London, John Frost, a Newport magistrate, was elected chairman. Representatives for the West Riding of Yorkshire were lawyer Feargus O'Connor, Bradford beer-house keeper Peter Bussey and Lawrence Pitkeighly, the general trader from Huddersfield. This was, potentially, a great moment in British history. It is a moment when, for the first time, political representatives of the working people had come together as a national body sufficient to make a difference. But, although it knew the potential of the labour power at its command, this Chartist Convention was an entity unknown to itself.

What would the men of the Chartist National Convention make of their creation? How could pressure best be put on the government for acceptance of the petition, and what should be done if the petition were rejected? Economic measures which included making withdrawals from savings banks, the boycotting of shops which were not Chartist-friendly and refusing to buy liquors taxed by the government were suggested and in some areas tried; and gatherings of vast numbers of people were organised to demonstrate working class solidarity and to spread the Chartist word.

On the 21st of May 1839, another huge public demonstration took place at Peep Green. More flags, more bands. Skircoat Green teenager, Benjamin Wilson, joined the throng for the first time. Benjamin Wilson was introduced to Chartism by an aunt of his at Skircoat and as he had 'many a time ... known what it is to be short of something to eat',[49] Chartism seemed to his young mind to be a good idea. '[W]e joined the procession in Halifax', he writes, 'and marched by Godley Lane and Hipperholme, at which place the Queensbury procession joined us'.[50] Speakers on the hustings that day were William Thornton of Bradford; Thomas Vevers, Lawrence Pitkeighly and George Barker of Huddersfield; Abraham Hanson of Elland; Feargus O'Connor and James Bronterre O'Brien; George White of Leeds; and from Barnsley, William Ashton, Peter Hoey and Joseph Crabtree. Mr. Martin represented Wakefield.

The atmosphere was not the same as the year before. Feargus O'Connor referred to the difficulties the organisers had had in challenging the authorities' view that the meeting was an illegal one. If soldiers had attended and fired upon them, he had determined that, 'no house should have covered his head that night'; he would have repelled, 'attack by attack', he said. Then he stepped aside for his colleague, James Bronterre O'Brien.

'Men of the West Riding of Yorkshire', Bronterre O'Brien began, 'I have come from Manchester this day to ask you one question, and that is, are you up to the mark?'. The Chartist 'mark' was a nebulous concept. He did not want them to use physical force in their struggle for the vote, but they might be driven to it. The one advantage working people had over the ruling elites was their overwhelming numbers, and if the authorities did not willingly give them a vote, military oppression would be the only way for the government to maintain its present system. 'The option is Universal Suffrage or military despotism ...' You must make a challenge, he told the crowd, you must represent a threat to compel the government to give way to your demands. In similar vein, Lawrence Pitkeighly said things had now reached a point where the authorities were wise enough not to obstruct them because, 'they knew the determination of the people too well for that'. And Peter Bussey reminded everyone that they had a constitutional right to arm just as the government armed the military, and that it was a, 'false libel on the people of England, that they wanted to destroy property; they were not such fools as to destroy that which they had created by the labour of their own hands'.[51]

Arm on the one hand, keep the peace on the other. The notion, 'Peaceably if we may, Forcibly if we must', became the slogan of the Chartist movement. It was necessarily ambiguous. One who knew Feargus O'Connor but was not a great admirer said O'Connor's 'few weak moral force professions were regarded as nothing more than the remaining remnants of his prudence, to be cast aside whenever circumstances might favour a bolder policy'.[52] Quite how the great crowds of working people took the Chartist orators' allusions to insurrection is a moot point. Some would understand it as an oratorical device, others, perhaps, might take what they heard more literally. Convention members who thought aggressive rhetoric to be a mistake on the part of men like Feargus O'Connor, James Bronterre O'Brien, George Julian Harney and Peter Bussey, resigned their Convention seats.

There was, however, to be no equivocation on the vote. It must be universal, no partial or extended vote would do. 'The cry of household [partial] suffrage might be raised by the enemies of the people', Feargus O'Connor is reported to have said, but if partial or extended was agreed upon by the Convention and by the people, then he would, at that moment 'leave them, and raise the shout of universal suffrage by himself'.[53]

Strikes were another way to put pressure on government and employer but to strike in these years was not the same as to strike today. Then it was raw. Could striking families survive beyond the first week? Would it keep the Chartist movement within the realms of legality? As the country was in a state of economic depression and the manufacturers less concerned to maintain full-out production, would a strike really hurt those at which it was aimed? Feargus O'Connor, James Bronterre O'Brien and others, did not like the idea of a strike because they judged the people unready to mount an effective one. A strike by an unprepared populace would only produce an unequal clash by pike-wielding workers against the nation's military with horses, rifles, cannon and sabres. There would be a bloodbath in the towns, failure to its instigators and punishment for its survivors. Feargus O'Connor, although alluding in his speech-making to the possibility of physical force and strike action, would not be responsible for their actuality. His National Convention would *follow* after the thing was done.

Imagine standing in the shoes of the politicised working man and woman in 1839. What was their thinking? It would be something along the lines of: we have a People's Parliament in the Chartist Convention; we are ill-used by our employers and the national government; we are starving and ready to act; what are we waiting for? Feargus O'Connor's reply to this kind of thinking was, to quote him, 'If you persevere I will go with you ...

> but reflect upon the advice which I give, when a struggle is to be made, even legally, it must be simultaneous. The whole cause should not be jeopardized by partial display'.[54]

All this while people were encouraged by what was written in the *Northern Star* and inspired by what they heard from Chartist orators. There is no obvious record of disquiet among the Halifax miners at this time, but miners in the South Wales coalfields were now ready to take matters into their own hands. Packages of guns, sent from Birmingham, were said to be arriving at Newport in South Wales[55] and their Chartist leaders, most prominent among them fifty-five-year-old John Frost and twenty-six-year-old Henry Vincent, were very actively travelling in that area, lecturing and challenging the authorities. Working men at Bradford practiced military drills on Fairweather Green, on the Thornton road. 'We won't be holding peaceable meetings much longer' said one Bradford man,[56] and one Halifax magistrate, quite obviously alarmed at what he was hearing from local authority informers, wrote, 'there are parties in various parts of our neighbourhood not only in possession of arms, but undergoing drill ... they are prepared to amend their condition at the expense of the community when called on by their [Chartist] leaders'.[57] And while all this was going on, on the first day of March 1839, eleven-year-old Joseph Grey was killed when a weight of stone fell on him from a pit roof at Southowram.

In April, in response to the swelling Chartist movement, the British Government appointed General Charles Napier as Northern District army commander in readiness to meet any insurrectionary action by the working people. Now a man of fifty-seven years, Charles Napier settled himself in at Nottingham in preparation of what might come. Meanwhile, Henry Vincent was tirelessly lecturing in South Wales, Herefordshire and Gloucestershire. Although on the one hand Henry Vincent had 'warned and cautioned the people ... to beware of men who council violence', on the other he did not 'object to arms', his only fear was 'an improper or a premature use of them'.[58] The aristocracy, he told his audiences, 'will not come down, they will be brought down, to their sorrow', and then, like so much Chartist rhetoric, was added, 'Will you keep the peace, in the event of a disturbance?' 'We will!', his audience cried ...

> Will you protect the life and property of all individuals of whatever political creed? ('We will!'). I shall then consider you as special constables. If your magistrates will not keep the peace ... lay hold of them, and put them in a coal-hole'.[59]

This kind of speech-making was too much for the authorities and Henry Vincent became the first Chartist Convention delegate to be arrested. Having gone to London in May, to participate in the collection of the petition and its handing over to the men who would present it to Parliament, he was taken into custody there by Tredegar police superintendent William Homan on an authority from the Newport magistrates for 'riotous assemblage'. In reaction came a truly riotous assemblage at Llanidloes in Wales, during which a number of local men were arrested. Up in Halifax, on Saturday 18th May, and totally obscured from public sight, a ten-year-old boy, Charles Cheatham, was killed in a Southowram mine from a fire damp explosion.

In Lancashire, a secret meeting took place between General Napier and the Chartist leaders there. Charles Napier represents an interesting archetype, that is, someone who had great sympathy with the cause of the working people, but stood against it. At this clandestine meeting he is reported to have said to the Chartist organisers of the May meeting on Kersal Moor,

> I will take care that neither soldier or policeman shall be within sight to disturb you. But meet peaceably, for if there is the least disturbance, I shall be amongst you and at the sacrifice of my life, if necessary, do my duty. Now go and do yours.[60]

This approach was typical of the official line. The government knew perfectly well that if it excited the working people beyond their endurance, something more than great assemblies and sporadic rioting would be the result. 'The first cannon which might be fired on the people will ignite suddenly all the property of the country', agreed Feargus O'Connor.[61]

On 14th June 1839, the great collection of all the many petitions which had been signed across the country in the past few months and now huge in size, was carried into the Houses of Parliament. It was presented there by Birmingham banker, economist and veteran campaigner for parliamentary reform, Thomas Attwood. When they saw it, some members laughed at the size of it and, in July, they rejected the petitioners, some 1,300,000 people, by 235 votes to 46. Many Chartist leaders had foreseen this result, but the people had not. It is said that, 'despair was diffused like a pestilence' among them.[62] So ended the Chartists' political hopes, at least for now.

Parliament's response to the Charter was a bold one for every man of sense must have appreciated the atmosphere of threat in the country. At Birmingham, on the evening of 15th July after earlier disturbances, a great crowd marched through Digbeth and destroyed property on its way to the Bull Ring where the destruction continued. With unrest fomenting, the Chartist Convention, also meeting at Birmingham, now called for a strike, often referred to as 'A Sacred Month', to begin on 12th August. It was called-off after just a few days. The Convention did not know what to do with the opportunity before it. Feargus O'Connor, a lawyer and aware of the delicate legal standing of the Chartist organization, hedged around the strike issue and eventually suggested that 12th August, rather than being a definite date, might be regarded, after all, as a provisional date for a strike. If the Chartist movement ever was a young stallion, this is the moment of its gelding.

At Halifax, Benjamin Rushton also advised caution when considering a strike. There was more than one Chartist meeting at Halifax, at their room on Jail Lane, to consider the wisest course to follow. It was found that a great many felt ambiguous about strike action.[63]

August came and it was a wet month. There was a great flood at Rotherham. On 6th August 1839 the Chartist Convention, now back in London, thought it would be better to have, not a strike but instead a stoppage of two or three days. It was a case of measuring strength. The government knew its strength, but the Chartist Convention did not know just how strong it might be, was possibly afraid of its strength, afraid of failure, of making matters worse, and was in some discord. Charles Napier's belief that it needed only the word from the Chartist leaders for insurrection to begin, had the leaders had the will, is a view as valid as any could be. While the Convention wavered on the brink, the government waded in. Following Henry Vincent, more arrests were made. The Chartist National Convention had great momentum at this point, but it vacillated. It is understandable. Much of its power was based in the provinces and without London no physical force actions were likely to bring results. A fatal lack of decisive leadership did two things. It rocked confidence in the Convention, and in the end it actually produced exactly what it most feared; it left insurrectionary attempts in the hands of small faction groups which were, indeed, doomed to fail.

Bradford had taken the strike action to its heart and so, at a meeting at Butterworth's Buildings, Peter Bussey had to give the frustrating news that the strike had shrunk to a stoppage of a few days.[64] At Halifax, when the stoppage day of Monday 12th August dawned, more than three hundred people in support of it turned up at the Jail Lane building where Thomas

Cliffe, Benjamin Rushton and his close friend Robert Wilkinson met and spoke to them.[65] In the rest of the country things were not so calm. Across the Pennines at Manchester, Bury, Bolton and later Rochdale, failure and indecision had agitated people so much that disturbances took place over the next few days. Magistrates read the Riot Act. This gave local authorities the power to demand a crowd to disperse within the hour, failure of which could lead to legal execution there and then on the street, or later through a court of law.

While this was going on, other lives were more privately playing out. On 23rd August Halifax's workhouse Guardians arranged for an elderly inmate to be removed, at his own request, to Manchester where his daughters lived. He was too ill to walk, 'so it was decided that he be wheeled in a barrow to the wagon which would take him across the Pennines'. He died on the road.[66] And up in Boothtown, Patience Kershaw's father was showing sign of illness. So slipped away the Sacred Month of August, 1839.

In September, seven months after its inaugural meeting, the Chartist Convention, unhappy with its own performance, dissolved itself. A major moment, if not the critical moment, had been left to pass by but in the towns hearts had been fired, hope raised, the will had been inspired. Significantly, some of the movement's leaders, now without a body to adhere to, met at Heckmondwike on Monday 30th September, at Mark Halliday's beerhouse in the Market Place.[67] Included in this eight-man faction group that day were Lawrence Pitkeighly of Huddersfield, T. Kitchingman of Halifax and Bradford's Peter Bussey. They resolved, unanimously, that 'Mr. O'Connor' should consider 'sending out missionaries to agitate the country, in preference to the payment of thirteen members to sit in Convention, we being of the opinion that such Convention can be of no service at present'. They also unanimously resolved that the power of the people's oppressors 'is fast approaching its dissolution, and that the people are ripe for a change'.[68]

Historians believe this meeting was called because it was known by these men that an uprising was being planned in South Wales and the idea to extend it to Yorkshire was their object. Certainly, the Monmouthshire miners and ironworkers had had enough and were preparing, in great secrecy, for action. Newport was to be their target.

The Newport leader, John Frost, found himself leading what might reasonably be described a revolutionary force which was rapidly gaining momentum.[69] Earlier, he had advised his Convention colleagues that the people in South Wales were beyond pacification and, the Charter rejected, the Convention dissolved and the political option gone, it was physical force which now offered itself as the only way forward. Five days after the Heckmondwike meeting Feargus O'Connor, through prudence or good fortune, quit Leeds for Ireland.

5

The Risings of 1839 -1840

On 9th October 1839, eleven-year-old James Jenning was killed in a Northowram mine from a fall down a shaft. He had been attempting to ascend the shaft without a corve. Although unreported in the local papers, Patience Kershaw and her family would very likely have heard of it. The mining community was a world unto itself. Feargus O'Connor wrote of it, that, '[e]very man who has taken an active part in Chartist agitation is aware that the non-adoption of Chartist principles by the colliers has long been a source of deep regret; in fact, that the colliers were not only not friendly to Chartist principles; but, on the contrary, were opposed to them, or heard them expounded with apparent indifference'.[70]

The colliers were the body which precipitated the revolts of these years but until the miners could emerge from their mental underground terrain, it was largely left to the men and women of the cloth and other manufacturing industries, to the trades and to the small establishment owners like Peter Bussey and Lawrence Pitkeighly, to constructively agitate for reform through the Charter. The miners, indifferent to formal politics, reacted more directly.

Peter Bussey, along with the South Wales miners' Chartist representative John Frost, and Huddersfield's Lawrence Pitkeithly, were billed to give a lecture at the theatre at Halifax on 21st November 1839. This public notice seems to have been displayed as a ploy to give the national authorities an impression of normality and to obscure John Frost's abnormal activities which, just then, were in the cause of the South Wales uprising. In any event, he did not turn up at Halifax on the 21st to give his lecture for the simple reason that, by then, he was under arrest for treason.[71]

In deep secrecy the South Wales miners and ironworkers planned their rising throughout the late summer and early autumn of 1839. These men, unlike weavers and combers, were very familiar with violent work. The Charter, they had been told, would be theirs within a month from the rising and the depth of their commitment is clarified in one miner's reported statement to John Frost six weeks before the event. This man had been a soldier, had fought at Waterloo and knew his business:

> I will tell you, Mr. Frost, the condition upon which my lodge will rise, and there is no other condition, as far as I am concerned ... I have been sent here to tell you that we shall not rise until you give us a list of those we are to remove – to kill. I know what the English army is, and I know how to fight them, and the only way to success is to attack and remove those who command them – the officers and those who administer the law'.[72]

Here is a straightforward statement of practical revolutionary tactic. As a method it was there for the taking and seems to have been part of the plan in the minds of many. It is a method which was not applied and which would have horrified John Frost. Here, laid before him, were the contents of the Pandora's box which he had opened.

The lead now being given by the miners and ironworkers of Monmouthshire was the response which the Chartist leaders had ostensibly been waiting for and yet John Frost was now describing himself as 'a doomed man'.[73] He was, 'pale, haggazed, much fatigued, and evidently dispirited'.[74]

The plan was to start with the taking of Newport, John Frost's home town, after which the industrial towns of Yorkshire would follow. But now, on the very eve of the uprising, Peter Bussey at Bradford had serious second thoughts. Having up until this time espoused and encouraged all things radical and revolutionary, he sent a courier to John Frost asking for a ten day delay to the uprising because Yorkshire, he explained, was unprepared. Some say 'Fat Peter' was a traitorous coward but he might, just as easily, have been a man of good sense as time would prove how hopeless the Welsh action was.

After an entire night of marching towards Newport, five thousand, 'drenched, begrimed, fatigued and many apparently frightened' men went down into the town in bright sunshine at nine o'clock on the morning of 4th November 1839. Despite their exhaustion, they raised a cheer as they went.

Nearly all were armed with rough weapons, some with guns.[75] One of them, George Shell, an eighteen-year-old utterly committed to the Chartist uprising, had written to his parents that night:

Dear Parent, [sic] - I hope this will find you well, as I am myself at this present. I shall this night be engaged in a glorious struggle for freedom, and should it please God to spare my life, I shall see you soon; but if not, grieve not for me, I shall have fallen in a noble cause. Farewell![76]

George Shell believed great change was at hand. The insurrectionists made their way directly to the Westgate Hotel where Newport's mayor, Thomas Phillips, and soldiers of the 45th Regiment awaited them. With barely a hesitation they attacked the building. Inside, Thomas Phillips ordered the soldiers to load and for the window shutters to be raised so that the men outside could be fired on. Within moments two attackers were dead on the street. Once inside the building, many more were killed as they tramped through the smoke filled hall and passageway, pikes held vertically as they went.[77] Reports tell that at least twenty insurrectionists died that day, instantly killed or fatally injured within the ten minutes it took for the soldiers to decisively bring an end to the attack. Included in the dead was the young cabinet maker from Pontypool, George Shell.[78]

This terrible event was exactly what the Chartist leaders had wanted to avoid but in some manner had inspired. News of this made its way to Yorkshire over the next few hours and put a stop to any notion of uprising there, at least for now. The authorities at Bradford sought permission to enclose Fairweather Green which functioned as a traditional Radical meeting place and exercise ground, intending to close it off for this purpose, and government spies continued to circulate in the city.[79]

In the week following the Newport uprising, two men were killed in a mine at Tredegar; men who very likely had marched with John Frost on the night of Sunday 3rd November. Four weeks after this, on 6th December, Joseph Brook, a boy of thirteen years, was killed by the collapse of a mine's tunnel roof at Bradford.

'It was known here (amongst the Chartists alone, of course) when the attack was to have been made, if successful a similar movement would have been attempted here', wrote James Stansfeld, a Halifax man destined to be one of the town's MPs.[80] One of those Chartists, John Snowden, recalls the night of the Newport uprising. "I well remember Sunday evening, November 3rd, 1839" when, he says, he was seated …

> with about twenty others, on benches in a cottage house in Street-bottom, Queensbury, at near midnight; and very vividly I call to mind the late Mr. Christopher Shackleton rising and saying, 'At this very moment, Frost is leading thousands of Welshmen to Newport to attempt once for all to establish the Charter by force of arms; and we who are here ought to have been doing our part in the same way, and would have been had not Bussey, who was to be our leader, wriggled himself out of the obligation into which he had entered by feigning sickness, prompted thereto by cowardice and treachery'.[81]

Peter Bussey had, indeed, lost all heart for a rising, even before the Newport attempt had been made. Like John Frost, his appetite for action of that magnitude was not as strong as it was in those he was supposed to lead. Bradford intended to follow after the Newport uprising and plans were laid there and at Halifax for that purpose, but now that it was upon them, and the first blow made, unsuccessfully, at Newport, Peter Bussey disappeared from his home. 'Some men' said his erstwhile colleague Henry Hodgson, 'had made long speeches … and then deserted'.[82] Bussey's excuse for not coming up to the mark at the appointed hour was ill health. His colleagues looked for him and when it was clear to them that he really had deserted the scene, they went again to his house where his young son let it be known, now his father was safely away, that he had been hiding: 'you could not find father the other day, but I knew where he was all the time, he was up in the cock-loft behind the flour sacks!'[83]

Meanwhile, John Frost had been pursued by the authorities and arrested shortly after the assault upon Newport. A December date was set for his trial for high treason. The Newport rising was a tragic event but some in Bradford and Halifax were not completely disheartened by it. They continued in their plans to rise up following Newport in spite of its failure.

'Dear Sir', wrote Halifax magistrate John Rhodes Ralph to Colonel Wemyss at Manchester on 12th November, nine days after the Newport uprising. '... you expressed a wish to be appraised of any expected movement of the disaffected in our neighbourhood ... There is a large room in this town used by the Chartists for their meetings ... Last Sunday evening my informant went out of curiosity and got admitted and staid there nearly three hours ... From the expressions of speakers, their idea was to "go to work" (meaning an outbreak for the purpose of plunder) and to do it in a better fashion than it had been done in Wales which they considered to have been sadly mismanaged'.[84]

The Halifax Chartists' plan, according to John Ralph's informant was to send a force from Ovenden, 'the worst we have', Ralph says, to join others and march to Bradford. The Halifax magistrates had learned that Chartist supporters 'are busy grinding their pikes and casting balls ... it will be unwise to overlook such symptoms as we recognise here'.

Apart from the apprehension and charging of fourteen men by James Feather, one of Halifax's police constables, for an attack on the house of Samuel Oliver on 16th November, nothing dire occurred at Halifax at this time.[85] At Bradford, the town's magistrates contacted the Home Secretary, Sir James Graham, to tell him that, '[a] large number of the adherents of the Chartists are under Arms and [the special constables] have nothing to oppose to them but staves'. They went on:

> we are further informed, indeed we know, that the peaceably disposed
> Inhabitants of Bradford in consequence of the frequent and unexpected
> Meetings of numerous assemblies of people who listen to and are
> excited by the Violent harangues of evil disposed and Revolutionary
> speakers are in the utmost alarm.[86]

Contemporary reports state that Bradford men approached at least one local gunsmith for large numbers of arms and at Shipley, Joseph North's smithy was producing spears with hooks to each side for the purpose of cutting the bridle reins of mounted soldiers and the yeomanry.[87] There is evidence of intent, but, significantly, it took a few weeks before anything resembling an uprising happened. The last two months of 1839 remained reasonably peaceful.

December arrived. It was a surprisingly mild month which was not good for Halifax because typhus broke out in the town. Typhus requires dirty living conditions and Halifax was certainly dirty. The average annual mortality rate was equal to one in forty of inhabitants according to a retrospective report of 1850; a rate which suggests that living and working conditions at Halifax were worse than in similar towns.[88] And the drainage system was terrible. One open drain, which ran from Trafalgar at King Cross down Savile Road and Hunger Hill before emptying its sewage and industrial waste into the Hebble Brook at the foot of Southowram hillside, grew steadily more foul from 1839. Another open drain in the town centre, on Crown Street, ran within twelve yards of one gentleman's living-room and gave off 'a very unpleasant smell'. Sewers on Cheapside, close to the surgeon James Holroyd's premises, and on Wade Street, were a deepening problem to residents, the Wade Street sewer being 'on a level' with one man's kitchen sink.[89] This foulness was concentrated in the town, and the warm late autumn of 1839 would not make Halifax any healthier. Patience Kershaw and her family were in a good place, high up there in Boothtown countryside where it was relatively clean.

Also in December, because of the social threat, thirty-six Dragoons had been billeted at Halifax, along with their horses. These soldiers' accommodation was arranged by the Halifax magistrates in scattered style, amongst various households, which gave townspeople the idea that they were the cause of the fever's spread in the town. Their billeting arrangements also made these soldiers vulnerable to attack. 'Fifty resolute Chartists', Charles Napier wrote from Nottingham, 'might disarm and destroy the whole [regiment] in ten minutes; and believe me, gentlemen, that a mob which has gained such a momentary triumph is of all mobs the most ferocious'.[90]

Then reports suggest the credulous belief that these soldiers would defect to the Chartist side when the insurrection came.[91] At Sheffield and Dewsbury coordinated plans were laid for a 'Rise' in the spirit of Newport. It is important to remember that, at this time, local Chartist groups had no

Convention to lead them. Samuel Holberry, a twenty-six-year-old Sheffield man and recently married, was the leader of this plan which he fixed for 31st December. 31st December is a significant date. It was the day on which John Frost's trial was to begin at Monmouth, and every Chartist sympathiser in the country was waiting for it.* Support funds were raised for John Frost, and action was anticipated by some, especially once judgement was passed. Samuel Holberry advised his men to prepare for the revolution by putting two shirts on to keep warm and to 'save every halfpenny … . to provide a Sixpenny dram as probably it would be very cold' on the night of the uprising.[92]

Meanwhile, at Bradford, a spy for the police, James Harrison, reported to Bradford's magistrates:

> On the 5th Dec. […] I was going from Bradford to the Queen's Head in company with George Flinn who is one of the Chartist Delegates. I said to him what do you think about this matter, what will it come to? He said it will come to something very serious in a short time, as the time is nearly at an end, meaning Frost's trial.[93]

Three weeks later, in January, 1840, news of the judgment on John Frost arrived at Halifax. At the time, John Snowden was attending an Anti-Corn Law meeting at the Odd Fellows' Hall at Halifax. It was common practice in these days for Chartists to attend the League's meetings in order to challenge their views. The building of the Odd Fellows' Hall was so new that it still had not officially been opened; in fact the ceiling plaster was yet to be applied. The building stood on St. James's Road and, with its massive Corinthian styled frontage, was a grand sight. Mill owner Jonathan Akroyd was chairing this meeting when William Cockroft unexpectedly entered, 'apparently much agitated'. William, known familiarly as Bill, had run the hundred yards or so up from the Chartist room in Jail Lane. "Mr Chairman", he gasped:

> "I don't come here to offer any opposition to your proceedings, nor to

---

* Also on trial with John Frost were the two other leaders of the uprising, William Jones and Zephaniah Williams.

the object this meeting has in view; but simply to say that The Times newspaper has just arrived, and it records that the jury at Monmouth have found Frost, Williams, and Jones guilty; and I propose that three dismal groans be given for that jury".[94]

'Three of the most dismal groans I ever heard were given', said John Snowden. John Frost had been found guilty, on Thursday 9th January 1840, of high treason and sentenced to death. The next night, Friday night, Halifax's magistrates panicked and called out the soldiers and special constables when they heard rumours of a possible combined reprisal attack on the town from Queenshead, Ovenden and Bradford, but no attack came.[95] Sheffield and Dewsbury rose up two days later, on Sunday the 12th.

At Dewsbury, in the very early hours of Sunday morning, a large group of men and women gathered on the outskirts of the town and fired off some shots which were answered from other groups farther off. They set a fire balloon off into the night sky to alert these other groups in outlying districts that the time was come to join together and descend upon the town, but the balloon burned itself out before reaching sufficient height and so the two hundred men and women who appeared in the town armed with 'pikes, pistols and bayonets' represented a diminished force. They stayed there until about three-thirty that morning, when they returned to their homes. One reporter later said:

> It is surprising that no more mischief was done. The whole of our police force being three, a constable (who is strongly suspected of being a Chartist himself), and two deputies.[96]

The Sheffield and Dewsbury disturbances, which had been intended as uprisings in the minds of their organisers, were quickly over. Samuel Holberry and his wife, Mary, were arrested at their home at 19 Eyre Lane in Sheffield, where daggers, a pistol, hand grenades, fire balls to be thrown, ball cartridges, bullets and other combustible materials were found.[97] Samuel Holberry was later imprisoned at Northallerton where conditions were dreadful. He was put to the treadmill.

After this, and in despite of the false alarm of the night of Friday

10th January, Bradford was still expected to rise. The magistrates and town's people were on tenter-hooks. 'Considerable alarm existed in this town on the nights of Saturday and Sunday, owing to reports that the Chartists at Clayton Heights and neighbourhood, intended to rise and make an attack on the town'.[98] Bradford's rising still did not happen for another two weeks, when an attempt was made by a number of men despite the lessons learned at Dewsbury and Sheffield. There also were reports that 'Peter Bussey, whose scarcity has been so much noticed lately', had returned to Bradford.[99] But it was not Bussey who led the Bradford uprising of January 1840. Robert Peddie was the man. Robert Peddie was not a native of the town. In fact, he had arrived there only a few days before, presumably with the intention of leading the rising.

At eight o'clock on the evening of Sunday, 26th January 1840, Robert Peddie, dressed in 'a drab great [coat], and a broad-brimmed hat, with a red comforter round his neck', met Isaac Holloway and George Flinn at their friend John Smith's house at Horton, on the road to Queenshead, in order to prepare weaponry and raise the men willing to join the insurrection which was to happen that very night.[100] Peddie's plan was to secure Bradford's piece-hall as a depot and then, once Bradford was taken, the body of his men would move on to Dewsbury and 'after taking Dewsbury they would take all the places on their way to London'.[101] There were, 'a hundred soldiers in Halifax', Robert Peddie said, 'who would be with them'.[102] They planned to 'obtain Cannon and Shells to meet the Military … and further to obtain possession of the Low Moor Company's Horses and Carts to be used for conveying necessaries, namely, shoes, clothes, Bread and Meat etc. For the Chartist army'.[103] The military magazine at Leeds was to be set on fire and the Chartists there brought to Bradford. It is very easy to see, in retrospect, just how unlikely to succeed this plan was, but to Robert Peddie and the working men who followed him it was a hope, it was all there was. The calculation did not go far.

At Halifax and Huddersfield some knew of the plan but, perhaps because they did not receive the messages from Peddie to join him, none reinforced his party at Bradford that night. More probably, no-one turned up because the rational-minded knew it was a plan not likely to succeed. Where were men like Benjamin Rushton at this time? Where were those like John Snowden and Lawrence Pitkeighly? These cultured working men were positioned between the Chartist leadership and the ground roots of the movement, the mass of working people. If they knew of Robert Peddie's scheme which, surely, they did, they would in all likelihood consider it a hopeless one. And they would be judging right. Their colleague, John Smith, in whose house Robert Peddie and the others were meeting, had no intention of joining them that night. 'I said I'm not going to rise – I advised them to stay at home'.[104]

Despite having accumulated an officially reported 500 guns, 500 pistols, 10,000 ball cartridges, 500 pikes, 500 swords and 500 daggers, the execution of the Bradford uprising amounted to little more than the seizing, in the very early hours of Monday 27th January, of a Bradford watchman after which men appeared on the Buttercross and in the Green Market where a second watchman was seized.[105] The Bradford authorities very quickly got things back to normal without a shot being fired, but during the whole of Monday 'the town continued in a state of feverish excitement ... The Court House presented the appearance of a place in a state of siege. Soldiers on guard, a six-pounder in front, and a large posse of special constables in and about the place'.[106]

Men like Robert Peddie and Samuel Holberry hazarded themselves in desperate fashion. The efforts of men like these produced for every one of them only imprisonment or exile; efforts which improved the condition of the working populations of Britain not at all. Hardly at all. Perhaps a little. It was a beginning. It was a beginning for which Samuel Holberry was to die in York Castle, on 21st June 1842. Supporters of Feargus O'Connor might have seen all this as proof of his prediction that action which is not wholesale will fail. And yet it was this say-it-but-do-not-do-it policy that encouraged willing men to take ill-considered action.

Less than one week after the Bradford disturbances, on 1st February 1840, John Frost's death sentence was commuted to life transportation by a canny government.

6
A Lull (1840-1841)

The great disturbances of the autumn of 1839 and early months of 1840 passed by. They meant a great deal to a great many. The British government had faced real insurrection; the working people had seen before them liberation in the Chartist movement. To Patience Kershaw's family, up at Boothtown, these events, perhaps, meant not so much. When news of the Newport uprising reached them, if it did, Patience and her siblings and mother, Elizabeth, had another matter on their minds. On Friday 1st November, three days before the men of Wales went into Newport, John Kershaw died. He did not die in the mine but in his own cottage on Plough Croft Lane, of liver disease. It can reasonably be assumed that John Kershaw was a typical, hard-drinking Yorkshire miner. He was fifty-nine years old at the end, and his death certificate appears to be the only official document on which his name was ever written. He probably worked down a Northowram coal mine for fifty years or more.

On 17th March 1840, Feargus O'Connor was found guilty at York of seditious libel for a speech of his own and for publishing, in the *Northern Star* eight months earlier, a speech made by William Taylor to the Manchester operatives which had been full of evangelical fire:

> I need not tell you that you are slaves, slaves bearing a great burden, slaves bearing a great load, slaves enduring great toil, slaves under the most oppressive system of government, and slaves that alone must work out their own freedom ... What are we to do, then? (Loud cries of 'Fight! fight! fight!')[107]

Also, in the week of William Taylor's speech, an eighteen-year-old apprentice called William Cockcroft ran away from his master, a shoemaker of Thornton, Bradford. William was five feet and four inches tall, he had lightish hair and a small lump on his jaw, also a broken tooth. He was full of face and, reportedly, bore a surly expression. When he ran away he was wearing a green coat and brown striped trousers. One guinea was promised to anyone apprehending and placing the boy in any of her Majesty's gaols until, like a slave, he could be reclaimed by his Bradford master.

In April, 1840, embellishments to the Odd Fellows' Hall at Halifax were completed and the ageing Robert Owen came to lecture there, for which event no less than three thousand people attended. There is no doubting that these personalities who carried the social message were regarded as the superstars of their day. Robert Owen was a philosopher as much, if not more, than a politician. He was a man of some spiritual beauty and believed in the spiritual beauty of others. Some called him a utopian, that he wasted his and everyone else's time on 'chimerical subjects'. Robert Owen sought social justice and a return to the dignity and independence which, before industrialisation, working people had enjoyed. His message to the people of Halifax would have been to encourage the establishment of colonies and cooperatives, where men and women could enjoy the fruits of their own labour — a New Moral World to accompany a New Moral Economy where wealth would be fairly redistributed. Robert Owen had been battling against Factory Slavery long before Richard Oastler became aware of it. '[B]ad and unwise as American Slavery is',

> the white slavery in the manufactures of England was at this unrestricted period far worse than the house slaves whom I afterwards saw in the West Indies and in the United States.[108]

It is reasonable to suppose that the Owenite Socialists, the Chartists and the Anti-Corn Law League might work together seeing that each was concerned to improve the lot of working people. Things are never that simple. From Leeds, the middle-class Anti-Corn Law Leaguers, through a newly formed Parliamentary Reform Association, were now making alliance overtures to the Chartists but the Chartists repelled them. For the Chartists' tastes, too many Anti-Corn Law Leaguers, those middle-class manufacturers and industrialists, were obstructing factory legislation, too many supported the New Poor Law and were pulling against the fight for a vote. What the Anti-Corn Law Leaguers really wanted, the Chartists believed, was workers with enough spare cash to buy their goods. And so the Chartists no more trusted the word of the middle-class Leaguers than did Richard Oastler. But

Richard Oastler was no Chartist. His concern was entirely with the fight against the New Poor Law and for the Ten Hours Bill. Robert Owen's Socialists were considered by just about everyone as impractical in concentrating on colonial or communitarian living. In their turn, the Owenites thought the Chartists were seriously mistaken in alienating the middle-classes!

One of Chartism's finest historians says, 'the Anti-Corn Law League claimed [that] repeal of the Corn Laws would bring down home food prices and thereby relieve distress without the need for an increase in wages', which was absolutely not what the Chartists wanted.[109] The Chartists and the Owenite Socialists were united in wanting to see a good day's pay for a good day's work and the restoration of a working family's independence and dignity. A meeting which took place in Huddersfield in January 1840 illustrates the problem very well.

At Huddersfield, just before the local uprisings of January 1840, Lawrence Pitkeighly went to hear the speeches of Sidney Smith, a man engaged by the Anti-Corn Law League to give lectures on their behalf. The hall was very crowded and a number of Chartists who had gone there with Pitkeithly suggested one of their own, Thomas Vevers, take the chair but were defeated in this, then one of them shouted out the name "Frost!", which produced return calls of "turn him out", from the Anti-Corn Law Leaguers. All taken in reasonably good spirit.

Sidney Smith, the Anti-Corn Law lecturer engaged for that night, explained to his audience that he calculated that back in 1835, 'sixty millions were spent in purchasing coats, hats, shoes, etc, which this year are totally and positively absorbed in the purchase of bread'. Everyone cheered this observation because everyone understood its meaning to themselves and to each other. For the Anti-Corn Law Leaguers this lack of spending power represented a danger to their trade, to the Chartists it was proof of the working people's dire condition in a time of unprecedented trade decline and wage reduction. Repeal the Corn Laws and trade will pick up, was Sidney Smith's message. Workers will be able to spend their money on more than just food and shelter; the entrepreneur will have his consumer.

Thomas Vevers argued, 'If we had been represented in the House of Commons, — if the House of Commons had been the people's house, as it ought to have been, we never should have had to have complained of a Corn Law'. An unassailable argument some might think, which Sidney Smith batted aside by saying that members of parliament have 'only to be stirred up with the long pole of public opinion' (cheers and laughter) 'in order to war as gently in favour of repeal, as a sucking dove' (more cheers and laughter). '[T]housands of poor persons are destitute; and if you only take advantage, master and man, with a long pull, a strong pull, and a pull all together, it is impossible but you must succeed'. (Cheers).

"Are we to conclude", Thomas Vevers asked, "that we are to obtain it [workers' prosperity] by physical force?" (Cries of "No"). "Let us know by what we are to gain it. We have petitioned times without number; and for want of the representation of the people, our petitions are disregarded ... It is ridiculous to petition a house that treats you with contempt".[110] And so the Chartists remained distinctly aloof from the Anti-Corn Law League. As far as they were concerned, the Leaguers represented the industrialists' vested interest which was bringing working families to their knees.

These political intrigues meant very little to the majority of miners in the vicinity of Huddersfield and Halifax. On 6th April 1840, William Marsden, a miner aged forty-two years and who, like John Kershaw, would have worked for decades in the mines, died in a gas explosion at Wyke. He had taken the top from his flaming lamp. And on 11th June, William and Joseph Sheard died in a mine at Halifax, also from a fire-damp explosion.

Despite all the recent disappointments and embarrassments of the previous twelve months, the Chartists rallied and from the ashes of the failed 1839 Convention the National Chartist Association was founded in July 1840. In this same month Richard Oastler was taken to court for non-payment of his debt to his former employer. He had run up debts in Thomas Thornhill's name to the huge sum of £2,000 and the court found against him. It was now left to be seen whether or not he could repay this debt. After five months it became clear that he could not, so he was sent to London's Fleet prison until such time as the debt could be paid. And Feargus O'Connor, after his conviction in March, was shut up in York Gaol. Two of the nation's leading social agitators were, thus, effectively removed from the scene for more than a year. To some, this would be a very satisfactory result.

Sunday 30th August 1840, was the day Patience's sister, Sybil, went with John Horsfall to Halifax's Parish Church to make her vows of marriage. This would be a simple ceremony for them. Registration shows that neither Sybil nor John could write their names. The dwelling in which they lived the following year suggests that both were workers at Crossley's Dean Clough mills which still stand where the Lee and Hebble Brooks meet, in the small vale separating the town from Haley Hill and which is spanned by the North Bridge. And in the next month the name of John Woodhead also was entered into the parish records, but not under marriages. Aged twenty-nine, he was killed when he fell from a corve while ascending a shaft in a Northowram mine.

7
Commission into Mines (1841)

It was viciously cold weather which brought in the New Year of 1841. In January, Halifax's Chartists found themselves homeless when their meeting place on Jail Lane was damaged by fire. They moved a few hundred yards up town to a room in Swan Coppice, where Halifax Town Hall now stands.

On 26th February Jonathan Sutcliffe died in a Halifax mine from a fire-damp explosion, and on 10th April, Mathew Smith died in the same way in a Northowram pit. Three weeks later marks the moment when Samuel Scriven arrived at Halifax charged with the task, by the Queen's appointed Commissioners, to collect information on Halifax's mining children:

> as to the time allowed each day for meals and as to the actual state, condition and treatment of such Children and as to the effects of such Employment, both with regard to their morals and their bodily health.[111]

The Commission had come about on the back of the ten year struggle, first of John Fielden and then Lord Ashley Cooper (later Lord Shaftesbury), to secure a minimum ten hour working day for mill workers. Both men had been recruited to the campaign in the early 1830s by the now imprisoned Richard Oastler. Working people had agitated for work-time controls for years and Lawrence Pitkeithly had supported Richard Oastler from the start. Lord Ashley tried for a ten-hour-day amendment to the existing, and toothless, Factory Act of 1833 and effective opposition to his efforts prevailed for a long time. Before parting company with the House of Commons in 1841, he managed to secure the appointment of the Children's Employment Commission. This Commission brought Samuel Scriven to Halifax in the spring of 1841.

Samuel Scriven and his wife, Caroline, stayed at the Northgate Hotel during their time at Halifax. A large troupe from an equestrian circus was staying there for some of the time also, stabling their horses in the large yard at the back of the building. Their presence must have brought tremendous light relief and colour to the sub-Commissioner between his visits to the local mines. He was greatly helped in his task by the Halifax surgeon James Holroyd, who knew the local mine and mill owners quite well. Most of Samuel Scriven's time at Halifax, though, was spent down coal mines. 'I soon found', he writes,

> from the difficulties I repeatedly experienced in bringing the children, who were especially objects of my search, from the mine to the cabins at the pits mouth, that my arrival in the district was pretty generally known and but little understood and all my endeavours to overcome the prejudices that evidently existed in the minds of the colliers proving fruitless, I determined at once to provide myself with a suitable dress of flannel, clogs and knee caps, in order that I might descend as many as possible, and take the dispositions of the children themselves during their short intervals of rest.[112]

Samuel Scriven crept on his knees, and crawled, 'like a turtle' he says, through tunnels of, sometimes, just twenty inches tall. He stretched out on flat boards, or was pushed in corves by willing hurriers, with his head hanging over one end, his feet over the other, all the time wondering if his body would clear the top of the tunnel. At Boothtown Pit, where Patience was working, he employed these techniques to get to the coal face and says that the 'bottom or floor of this gate was every here and there three or four inches deep in water, and muddy throughout'. He likened these kinds of tunnel, or gate, to city drains. The miners' appearance shocked him, here and everywhere. They lay, naked, on the tunnel floor and supported their heads upon a board or small crutch to work, or they hewed in a crouched position, sitting upon one heel and balancing themselves by extending their other leg forward. He was told that these men were 'mashed up' by their forties.

'The colliers', wrote one of the London Commissioners visiting Scotland, are 'a separate race, apart from the labouring masses'.[113] They were reckoned to be heavy drinkers inclined to lead an undisciplined and isolated life. And once a miner, always a miner. The Boothtown miners' lives differed from many in Scotland, Wales and the Midlands of England where the mining communities were often exclusive. The Northowram miners lived in close proximity to families of different trades who, in fact, outnumbered them. It had been calculated, ten years earlier, that across the 3,400 acres of Northowram, families working in trade, factories and handicrafts were eight times more numerous than those working in other industries, and were seventeen times more numerous than agricultural workers. In the small community of Boothtown itself were at least two boot and shoe makers, a clog and patten maker, shopkeepers, tailors, a wheelwright and at least one blacksmith's shop besides the outworkers to the Akroyd mills and Atkinson's silk spinning works.[114] Patience's family represented one of just two mining families living up Plough Croft Lane, the majority of households there were of the silk, woollen and cotton trade. Boothtown had its charity school for fifty boys and girls, also a public house called the New Inn.

Down in Halifax, the new workhouse on Gibbet Street, which had been open for fourteen months and was now buying its coal from Joseph Stocks at £13 in the summer quarter, apprenticed their children to miners when any individual applied for one. This was not unusual. Pauper and orphan children had been apprenticed by workhouses to the new factories in the industrialised areas for decades. The term 'apprentice' was an alternative term for something more like 'slave', and Samuel Scriven was about to hear of this slavery at first hand.

About two weeks after his meeting with Patience at the Boothtown Pit, Samuel Scriven spoke to a boy working at Isaac Wood's Pinchback Pit who did not know his own age. He knew his name though, which was Thomas Moorhouse. "I am a chance child" he explained to Scriven, "mother is dead also. I don't know how long she has been dead. 'Tis better na three years".

> I began to hurry when I was nine year old for William Greenwood. I was
> apprenticed and I lived with him … He was bound to find me victuals
> and drink and clothes but I never had enough. I used to have porridge
> and treacle and water and sometimes dry cake and coffee. William

Greenwood gave me a bed to lie upon. It was a chaff bed. Henry Grimes slept with me. That was his nephew. His own lad slept with us. We used to lie top o' tick without getting anything else and had an old blanket and ragged sheet over us. I used sometimes to go to bed, sometimes at eight o'clock or nine and got up at five, had my breakfast and went to work. We took dry cake with us nothing to drink. I ran away from him because he lost my indentures for he served me very bad. He stuck a pick into me twice in my bottom.

'Here I made the boy strip' writes Scriven, 'and found a large cicatrix likely to have been occasioned by such an instrument which must have passed through the glutei muscles and stopped only short of the hip joint'

He used to hit me so bad … that I left him and went about to see if I could get a job. I used to sleep in the cabins upon the pit's bank and in the old pits that had done working. I laid upon the shale all night … I [ate] for a long time the candles that I found in the pits that the colliers left over night … The rest of the hurriers did not know where I was. I got to Bradford after a while and had a job there for a month … I work now for John Cawtherly. He took me into this house and is serving me very well. I hurry now 15 corves a day over 200 yards, sometimes 20, sometimes 30.[115]

Miners were known to earn more, a little more, than their mill and agricultural counterparts. Patience's second eldest brother, William, at the age of twenty-two, was earning at this time sixteen shillings a week, out of which he must pay for candles, the purchase and sharpening of tools and his hurrier's wages, before meeting household expenses and rent. A miner ten years older, with a wife and three children, who worked at another of Joseph Stock's mines was earning just over £1 a week. At Joseph Stock's Lightcliffe mine, the youngest worker, who was eight years old and so almost certainly a trapper, earned two shillings a week so taking home enough to feed herself. Patience at sixteen years was earning eight shillings and six pence a week at Stock's Boothtown Colliery. This would be considered a good wage for a girl who seems to have been a strong and efficient worker.[116]

Samuel Scriven found that the child hurriers of Halifax were, indeed, muscular, but saw what James Holroyd, despite his medical training, did not, that the children were stunted in growth. Scriven attributed this to the 'severe labour exacted from them during a period of infancy and adolescence'. He took measurements from the children when he was with them in the mines and came to the conclusion that diminished height and exaggerated muscularity went together in young mine workers. Not he, nor James Holroyd were aware that, to quote Friedrich Engels who was collecting evidence on the condition of the working classes at this time, 'from the bad, dust-filled atmosphere mixed with carbonic acid and hydrocarbon gas, which might so readily be avoided, there arise numerous painful and dangerous affections of the lungs ... which appears in the fortieth, in others in the thirtieth year in most of the miners'.[117]

Samuel Scriven also was interested in the intellectual effects on the children of their daily twelve hours of extreme, physical work with rough miners in black tunnels. He took with him into the mines a child's reading book, and found, out of a sample of the two hundred and nineteen children with whom he spoke at the pits' bottom, that thirty-one could read 'an easy book' and just fifteen could write their names.

He also found that girls and boys did identical work. 'There is no distinction whatever ... in the weights of the corves or in the distances they are hurried, in wages or dress'. 'Indeed', he writes:

> it is impossible to distinguish, either in the darkness of the gates in which they labour, or in the cabins before the broad day light of day, an atom of difference between one sex and the other.[118]

The girls, he found, were as equally 'vulgar' and 'obscene in language' as the boys, and had nothing other than a 'ragged shift or in the absence of that a pair of broken trousers to cover their person'.

At Huddersfield he took one child up to the surface from Waterhouse Pit at Lindley to discover that it was a girl. 'Nothing that I can conceive amidst all the misery and wretchedness in the worst of factories [is] equal to this' he said. His companions, Mr. Brook, a surgeon, and Mr. Holroyd a solicitor, although 'living within a few miles' Scriven added, could not believe that such 'unchristian' cruelty could exist. The little girl was clothed in a rag 'which hung about her waist', and he took her with him to the nearest public house. They were followed there by one of the mine workers who, 'wanted to take her away because, as he expressed himself, it was not decent that she should be (her person) exposed to us'. 'Oh no!' wrote Scriven, 'it was criminal above ground and, like the other colliers ... he became evidently mortified that these deeds of darkness should be brought to light'.[119]

A potential fire-damp explosion nearly put an end to Samuel Scriven's experiences, at Halifax or anywhere else. In a tunnel at Wyke Lane Pit he became aware that there was a great deal of gas present and the boy who was leading him held up his Davey lamp to show him the blue flame burning there as proof. Then the boy made to blow at it through the gauze; a disastrous thing to do in a tunnel full of gas. Scriven grabbed for the lamp and actually struck it from the boy's hand which extinguished the flame. This saved their lives but now, in darkness so intense that it is properly described as pressing, they had to grope their way back the way they had come, all the time afraid they might meet an oncoming corve.

On 12th June, Samuel Scriven inspected Isaac Wood's Pinchback Pit when a boy was injured while being drawn up the shaft. The child died four hours later. A week after this, Scriven inspected his last mine and prepared to go home.

8

The 1841 Election and Chartist Revival

As June drew to a close, Samuel and Caroline Scriven returned to their home at Regent's Park in London and Scriven began the job of writing-up his report on what he had seen at Halifax and the things he had heard from Patience Kershaw and the other children encountered under the hills of Halifax and Huddersfield and at Low Moor. At the time of the Scrivens' departure from Halifax, General Napier quit Nottingham, his role as Northern Commander having come to a natural end. The fear of revolution was over for the time being and the Chartists, it seems, were defeated, despite the existence of the newly formed National Chartist Association. Hundreds of activists were in prison and many others had emigrated. Peter Bussey had taken off for New York.

'The Chartist agitation appeared to be crushed' wrote Benjamin Wilson some years after these events, 'and the people felt great disappointment, they really had thought they were going to accomplish all they were agitating for, and some began to despair that it would never be done'.[120] People like Patience and her sisters and brothers continued to work in the mills or down the coal mines under the conditions Samuel was about to expose and the owners continued to cut wages. The Anti-Corn Law League was as busy as ever in its campaign for repeal of the Corn Laws and occasionally Robert Owen's socialists caused disquiet among the respectable classes, not just for challenging the political but also the religious establishment. They were viewed as dangerous because they were Socialists and Infidels, but the Owenites never threatened violence.

1841 was a year of parliamentary elections. At Halifax, Benjamin Wilson thought this, 'the tamest election since the borough was enfranchised', but this election year reflected some interesting social changes. Only a tiny proportion of men was allowed to vote at it but, at Halifax, Liberals Edward Protheroe and Sir Charles Wood found themselves sharing the hustings with, and answering the questions of disenfranchised working men.

At Halifax, on nomination day, everyone gathered at the Piece Hall. John Crossland, as Halifax's handloom weavers' representative, mounted the platform erected in the central open space of the Piece Hall and stood beside the Liberal (Whig) candidate Sir Charles Wood to ask him why the government had not acted on the facts it had gathered, 'which gave them information of our distress'. Charles Wood's reply was to say that the, 'only measure that the hand-loom weavers can look to', was repeal of the Corn Laws. In the Piece Hall that day were many weavers and combers who perfectly understood the motivations of the Anti-Corn Law repealers.

John Crossland also wanted to know if Sir Charles would vote in parliament for the People's Charter if, 'requested to do so by a most numerously signed petition from the people of Halifax'. 'No,' replied the Liberal candidate, 'I won't vote for the People's Charter'. The crowd received this with loud groans. And when asked by Thomas Cliffe if he would vote for repeal of the New Poor Law, Charles Wood's answer was that he had seen the law 'attended with good effects'. The vast majority of those who heard him did not have the vote, so he knew he could safely be honest in his replies.

Benjamin Rushton also spoke from the hustings against huge government spending on a standing army which was retained, he said, 'to force the people to pay the national debt and taxes'. Then he, too, asked the Radical candidate Edward Protheroe if he would vote for repeal of the Poor Law. "I cannot vote for such a repeal", Protheroe replied, which brought forth more groans and cries of, "Over with him", from the crowd.

It was left to the Tory, George Sinclair, to declare his opposition to the New Poor Law and when the returning officer took a show of hands for the candidates from everyone gathered at the Piece Hall, four-fifths of hands were raised for Sinclair. 'Most tremendous shouts of applause followed the announcement'.[121]

'There was ... something heroic in the attitude assumed by working men' at this time, wrote an observer ten years after the event.

It was a battle of the employer and the employed. Masters were astonished at what they deemed the audacity of their workmen, who made no scruple of standing beside them on the platform, and contesting with them face to face their most cherished doctrines. Terrible was the persecution they suffered for taking this liberty. Loss of employment usually followed, but it was in vain that their employers endeavoured to starve them into submission ...[122]

The Liberals were defeated in the 1841 general election. The Tories were returned. It was a blow against the Anti-Corn Law League and the middle-class industrialist.

Although the 1839 petition had been roundly rejected by parliament, another was planned by the National Charter Association. Feargus O'Connor was not released from York gaol until August 1841, but as soon as he was, he began to campaign. At midday, on Wednesday 1st December 1841, he arrived at Halifax from Leeds via Sowerby Bridge railway station. It was a very cold day and he was greeted, to the astonishment of his fellow rail travellers, by thousands of people cheering as he got down from the train. The Halifax greeting party drew him in an open carriage from the station, up the hill and down again into Halifax Town, preceded by marshalls on horseback, accompanied by two bands and the thousands who had come to meet him. Together, all went down King Cross Lane, Cheapside, Corn Market, Crown Street, Old Market, Horton Street, along Church Lane, around the church then up to Woolshops, along Northgate, Broad Street, Waterhouse Street, Silver Street and Cow Green, before arriving at the Odd Fellows Hall on St. James's Road.

Throughout the entire route 'the middle and higher classes' who lived in the town centre, watched the parade from their windows and,

not the slightest expression of dissatisfaction escaped any part of the procession, as they passed the houses of their more violent political opponents; nor did any accident occur to mar the pleasure of the day'[123]

Inside the Odd Fellows' Hall tea was laid on for almost a thousand people after which the tables were removed so that another thousand could come in for the speeches. Everybody else was left to go home. Benjamin Rushton was asked to take the chair and a toast was raised, 'To the people, the source of all power', which was greeted with cheers.

When Feargus O'Connor came forward to speak, he was received with thunderous applause and cheering. 'The Corn Law Repealers ...' he said,

> now, after failing to sever us from our principles, are coming out for Universal Suffrage ... what respect can we have for those who have joined us at the eleventh hour ... They want neither household suffrage nor universal ... they wish only to take advantage of our movement to return the Whigs [Liberals] to power.

Loud cheers followed this. The 1841 election had been a shock to the middle-classes and the Chartists only despised them the more.

Another toast was made: 'May all the friends of liberty unite in one common band of brotherhood under the auspices of the people's selected plan', whereupon three cheers were given for the Charter. Feargus O'Connor proposed a vote of thanks to Benjamin Rushton, their 'veteran chairman', and then set about enrolling names to the petition.

The Year of Crisis

9
Exposure of Mine Working (1842)

And so arrived 1842. From his prison cell at the Fleet, in London, Richard Oastler had taken to writing open letters to his old employer, Thomas Thornhill. On the first day of 1842 he wrote,

> I am not a prophet, nor yet the son of one, but, judging from "the signs of the times," if I mistake not, this year will be one of unrivalled importance.[124]

It, perhaps, did not take prophetic sight to see that things were reaching a point of critical mass. Trade was very bad, workers' wages were withering away and work too. It is said that a hand-loom weaver earning a weekly sixteen shillings thirty years earlier, now was earning six shillings and six pence.[125] He had lost nearly two-thirds of his income during his working life. There was a threat of further wage cuts because of the downturn in trade. One cloth worker, who also was a prominent Chartist, said "the longer and harder I have worked the poorer and poorer I have become every year, until, at last, I am nearly exhausted".[126]

The year started slowly at Halifax. During February there was snow on the ground. The Halifax Workhouse Guardians advertised for a school master 'competent to teach reading, writing and arithmetic, and to train the children in industrious habits'. And then, at a meeting held on Wednesday the 24th, one of the Guardians, Abraham Pitchforth, moved for the dissolution of the Halifax Union and a return to the old system. 'The distance which the poor have to come' he said,

> the sacrifices the Guardians have to make in order to do imperfectly at Halifax what could be done twice as well, with half the trouble, in their own townships ... the unwieldy size of the Union, which prevent the Guardians from paying attention to the details of cases, and which [give] almost uncontrollable power to their paid servants, the relieving officers ...[127]

All these, Abraham Pitchforth believed, gave cause to rescind the decision made five years ago. The chairman, William Baxter, thought his colleague's proposal was contrary to the law, and it failed to pass.

1842 turned out to be a particularly fair year, a hot, sunny year. The second petition was presented to parliament on 2nd May, overseen by a London Convention consisting of twenty-five Chartists including, of course, Feargus O'Connor, James Bronterre O'Brien, also Lawrence Pitkeithly from Huddersfield. Before Thomas Slingsby Duncombe, MP for Finsbury, could present it to the house, the petition, which was huge and this time containing more than three million signatures, had to be broken apart before it could pass through the chamber door. These millions of petitioners were again rejected by 287 men over 49 in support. Thomas Slingsby Duncombe declared that he was so disgusted with the conduct of the House of Commons, 'that if the people ever got up another petition of the kind, he would not be a party to their degradation by presenting it ...'[128] The great People's Charter of 1842 was taken to the cellars and burned.

A local procession along the Calder valley which had preceded the petition's presentation had been a great deal hopeful of constitutional change, and the disappointment at learning how hopeless, in fact, it all was must have been dreadful to a great many.[129] The nail workers of Birmingham put down tools, there was a riot at Blackburn.

Then, on 14th May, *Halifax Guardian* readers, opening their papers, perhaps over their Saturday morning breakfasts taken long after Patience Kershaw had pushed her first corve of the day through Boothtown Colliery tunnels, saw this on page four:

> Yorkshiremen! – we ask of you in the name of mercy and of One whose attribute it is to be merciful, to read as calmly as you may, but read attentively, the epitome of evidence which we this day commence from the Report of the Children's Employment Commission ... Our abhorrence, together with that of many estimable men, had been fully excited by the recital of the cruelties and barbarities practiced on female slaves in a distant island, dreaming that not here – in our own island – women and girls hurry in coal pits "naked down to the waist" for men who work "stark naked, or with a flannel waistcoat only.[130]

Lord Ashley's Commission into child labour had published its findings, after some difficulty, and here it was for every man and woman to read. The article went on to describe what Samuel Scriven and his fellow sub-commissioners had unearthed during their time in Yorkshire; stories of girl hurriers 'dressed like boys' and 'crawling on all fours' with chains passing between their legs and hauling great weights of coal; stories of women giving birth in the pits and bring their new born up the shaft wrapped in their skirts. Stories of how six year old children could grow used to work which was beyond the imaginings of the most enlightened minds of these years, and of how 'a collier is a disabled man with the marks of old age upon him, when other men have scarcely passed beyond their prime'. The long article finished with the sentence, 'Is this in England?', and was immediately followed with a piece describing Queen Victoria's recent ball costume supporting, 'a pendent stomacher of the intrinsic worth of £80,000'.

The *Halifax Guardian*, a Tory paper, called on Ten Hour Bill supporters who were focused on mill working only, to join in condemning the employment of children and women in the mines. There was a great deal here to embarrass the Halifax mine owners and their families and more was to come. The following week appeared, on page five, a column headed:

WHITE SLAVERY IN ENGLAND

and quoted was Patience Kershaw's testimony given to Samuel Scriven.

The tone of conversation between Halifax mine owner and newspaper proprietor over these two weeks can only be guessed. The following week it was the turn of the miners to be shamed. Miners worked as self-employed men, as a type of freelance getter, which was an arrangement behind which the owners were able to hide themselves from responsibility. On 21st May, the 'main authors' of the cruelties perpetrated in coal-mines, the *Halifax Guardian* now says, 'are not the masters, nor their foremen, but the workmen themselves, the fathers or relatives of the children and women doomed to this heartless slavery.

> For permitting these things to be so in *their* mines, the masters are
> indeed reprehensible, even if they were ignorant of them, for what
> master ought to be ignorant of his own affairs? But after all it is the
> colliers who put their infants to such labour ...[131]

And turning the page from this article, the reader's eye fell upon drawings
made by Samuel Scriven during his weeks at Halifax. He was talented and
the pencil sketches he made of the hurriers he met were striking seen on the
broad pages of the *Guardian*. They impress in ways words cannot. Drawings
of naked boys thrusting and pulling loads along tunnels two feet high,
another of a girl pulling a load by a belt secured by chains which pass
between her legs, and one of a boy and girl, clinging together face-to-face,
legs akimbo, as they are drawn up the pit shaft on a catch-iron wound by an
old woman.

Judging from his report, Samuel Scriven did not agree with the
surgeon James Holroyd's general view that responsibility for safety was the
child's own. 'On perusal of the verdicts', he wrote of mining accidents, 'it
will be seen that in a large proportion of these cases the fatal results might
be obviated by precaution and care on the part of the proprietors and of the
colliers themselves'. It seemed to Samuel Scriven that a notion of
responsibility, the notion of guilt, if laid at the door of the proprietors and
miners, 'might be employed with effect in diminishing [accident] frequency'.
He perfectly understood that his report must be objective but he could not
restrain himself from this:

> ... this lead me to the consideration of the absolute indifference too
> frequently manifested by that class of persons whose care would be
> bestowed upon the improvement of the youthful population rising up
> about them. In proof of which it is only necessary to refer you to the
> evidence of Mr. Emmet and Mr. Rawson, junior ... [who] appear to
> attach to themselves neither responsibility or care so long as they enjoyed
> the comforts and affluence that [the miners'] daily toil brought them.[132]

The owners were at fault according to Samuel Scriven.

Three weeks after this shock to the senses of Halifax's respectable mine owners and their friends, came a shock to the town's Chartists. After serving just nineteen months of his four year prison sentence for inciting the Sheffield and Dewsbury uprisings of early 1840, Samuel Holberry, who had entered North Allerton prison as 'a very tall, well formed and muscular young man', died of consumption, aged twenty-eight, soon after being transferred to York Castle.[133] 'Poor, brave Holberry is dead', wrote Jonathan Bairstow to a friend.

> I received the astounding intelligence in a letter from York in the middle of a lecture last night – I was struck dumb – I staggered, my head reeled to and fro like a drunken man's – I felt mad – I spoke on for upwards of two hours – my God what an impression – the crowd meeting all seemed bursting – never such a feeling in the world did I see.[134]

Samuel Holberry was buried at Sheffield and it is said fifty thousand people paid their respects that day. George Julian Harney gave the oration.

And yet another mining incident occurred at Halifax in the second week of July, at a Northowram pit owned by Mr. Wilson, when miner Jabez Parker died soon after being struck by a large stone. An inquest found no responsibility attaching to anyone. The verdict on Jabez Parker was accidental death.[135]

As the respectable residents of Halifax were reading the shocking details of child labour taking place under the green and pleasant hills upon which they looked from their living-room windows, the House of Commons was voting on a proposal to suspend the new Poor Law. All but twenty-nine MPs rejected the idea. And Lord Ashley, his 1841 commissioners' reports now made public, was struggling to secure a date for his presentation to the House of Commons of his Mines and Collieries' Regulation Bill which proposed the prohibition of the working of children and women down mines. The next four weeks were full with obstruction from within the House by a government led by Robert Peel, a man himself a mine owner, and by demands from other powerful coal-mine owners for amendments to Ashley's proposals.

No assistance, no sympathy – every obstacle in the way, though I doubt
whether they will dare *openly to oppose* me on the Bill itself.[136]

wrote Ashley. He finally succeeded to get his Bill heard. On 7th June he
spoke with genius to the House of Commons for two hours and did not fail
to describe to the listening members ghastly instances of the brutal
treatment of children recorded by the sub-commissioners the year before.
Many were affected by what they heard. '[T]he success has been *wonderful,
yes, really wonderful*', he wrote in his diary two days later. But the Bill had
to be read three times in the House of Commons and then go to the Lords
before it could be made law. More fierce opposition awaited him. One
member, spuriously defending cruelty through the threat of more cruelty,
explained how the Bill's measure to prohibit the employment of children
and women in mines would mean that …

hundreds of children will be thrown out of employment, and hundreds
of families will be driven to the workhouses.[137]

Still the Bill survived. It came up for its final reading on 1st July. Four days
later, with two amendments now attaching to it, it was passed to the Lords.
Ashley was still far from confident of its success. 'Now I am impotent', he
wrote in mid-July, 'nothing remains (humanly speaking) but public opinion
– were it not for this I should not be able to carry *one* particle of the Bill …
It is impossible to keep faith with this Ministry, their promises are worth
nothing'.[138]

It was debated in the Lords on 24th July 1842 and the atmosphere
grew very heated. 'Never have I seen such a display of selfishness, frigidity
to every human sentiment, such ready and happy self-delusion', Ashley
railed in his diary. But the Bill passed, even if it was as a severely amended
one, and found its way onto the Statue Books on 10th August 1842. And so,
Lord Ashley did succeeded in stopping the employment of girls and women
down mines under this Act, but he also had wanted to ensure a ban on all
boys younger than thirteen years being taken underground to work. The age
restriction for boys was lowered to ten years. And he had wanted the
prohibition of anyone under the age of twenty-one being given responsibility

for the safe working of steam driven winding gear which was critical to safety. Under the amendments, this task was allowed to fifteen-year-olds. Also, he had sought to abolish apprenticeships of workhouse children. 'Let apprenticeship be abolished on the spot; let every existing indenture be cancelled', he had said. Under agreed amendments, this practice was continued to be allowed as long as a boy had reached his tenth birthday.

At Halifax, at the very time of the Bill's passing, a twelve-year-old boy, apprenticed out by the town's workhouse guardians to a miner, was taken to the magistrates' court at Ward's End by his master, Joseph Watson, for refusing to work for him. The boy explained that Joseph Watson, 'abused him and often kicked him'. When the magistrates John Waterhouse, John Rhodes Ralph and John Rawson said they would send him to the House of Correction for a month if he refused to return to his master, the lad 'softened ... and was obliged to be carried out of the court'.[139] According to *The Bradford Observer,* the child was committed to Wakefield for a month so, given the two options, he preferred the idea of imprisonment to life under Joseph Watson.[140]

As if the planets were come together, there were some observers who, like seers, could see the eruption ahead. In July, while Ashley was fighting for his Bill, Richard Oastler published from the Fleet Prison one of his flourishing open letters:

> It is true that "outside" misery abounds, and wretchedness, and woe, and want; and grim and ghastly death by hunger ... I guess the feelings thus betokened, nay, in this cell, can complete such scenes of woe, though, in mercy, the hearing and the sight are hindered by these high walls. I can feel as keenly now as I was wont to do when I prophesied all these things, and warned the affluent ... that such woes were hastening ... then I was sneered at! Yes, I *did* warn my countrymen, and, though unheeded, pointed the way to plenty, prosperity and peace.[141]

Richard Oastler saw, from his cell, what many free men refused to see. The working people had had more than enough.

In July colliers in the Black Country coalfield came out on strike because of wage reductions. Aggression shown towards strike breakers, 'blacklegs', at Parkfield colliery in violation of legislation designed to suppress this kind of behaviour was dealt with by the authorities as seditious and indictable. There were arrests and imprisonments.[142]

Then on Monday 1st August 1842, an extraordinary thing happened. Something 'most mysterious', the *Leeds Mercury* called it. On the streets of Halifax appeared hundreds of miners. They had come down from the North and Southowram hillsides of Halifax to the astonishment of the town dwellers who could not explain their appearance and had never seen anything like it. The miners had hired the Odd Fellows' Hall for their purposes which, the *Halifax Courier* said, 'could not be correctly ascertained, as reporters for the public press were studiously excluded ... [S]o careful were they lest their proceeding should come to the light, that they turned out all the stewards and banksmen who were present'. This meeting definitely was not one to which the owners' men were welcome.

> A "hole and corner" meeting of the colliers of this district was held in the Odd Fellows Hall, in the town ... We understand that delegates from several of the adjoining towns were present. The object of the meeting is suspected to be the formation of a general union, in order to raise a general strike so as to bring machinery and all power requiring coals to a stand. If so, we can assure the parties concerned, that they will soon find out their mistake.[143]

It is very likely that Patience Kershaw's older brothers, Thomas and William, were two of the miners who attended that day's meeting. It was an event which heralded the start of change.

10

The Great Strike Comes to Halifax (1842)

In this eighth month of 1842, an operatives' walk-out started what could be called the first national industrial strike in Great Britain, or anywhere else as far as it is known.[144] This, briefly, is how it happened:

The shortage of coal, due to the Black Country coalfield stoppage, led to lay-offs in the neighbouring Potteries. Then wage cuts were again threatened at the Lancashire cotton mills. Trade was so bad by now that, on 5th August, workers at Bailey's mill at Stalybridge, east of Manchester, were laid-off for a month with the news that they must also submit to a twenty-five percent wage reduction. Things had reached such a pitch that these workers refused to go back when asked. This was the day of the first, substantial, walk-out in the northern counties. Two days later, Sunday 7th August, a great meeting took place on Mottram Moor, south-east of Stalybridge, equidistant between it and Glossop, and the Chartists there were later charged with having incited more walk-outs for the next day.[145] And indeed, widespread walk-outs did happen the next day when, amidst some scenes of conflict, crowds of striking workers brought other operatives out from their mills. Two days later thousands upon thousands of workers marched into Manchester:

> [I]t was lead by a large party of young women very decently dressed. Both they and the men who followed were arranged in regular file, and nothing could be apparently more respectful and peaceable than their demeanour'.[146]

This was a very different crowd from the one which had descended upon Newport three years earlier entirely made up of armed men. Here we have women leading a multitude which marched in orderly fashion. But it did not remain quite so orderly. In the following days there was much disturbance at Manchester as more workers turned-out, or were turned-out. Those who had first struck were determined to bring out everyone else, not just of their own trade but of every trade, if possible. Manchester's magistrates manned the town hall, day and night for the next two weeks or more. They already had about five hundred troops for their defence and, after applying to London for more, 'we had ... perhaps about 1500, but I cannot speak with accuracy' said one magistrate.[147] In the midst of all this, Lord Ashley's Coal Mine and Collieries Regulation Act was passing its last hurdles in the Commons, while people came out onto the London streets to 'hiss and boo' the movement of troops northwards. Some Londoners called out, 'Remember, you are brothers'.[148]

Across Lancashire the strikers very quickly organised Committees of Public Safety, quasi-authorities alluding to the French Revolution's Committee of Public Safety, which assumed some powers of control over the general public. Some applied to these Committees for permission to finish work-in-hand. The sense of excitement and destiny must have been intense. The strikers began to move, as a body, towards Yorkshire.

The Chartists, who three years ago had anguished over calling for a strike, saw this workers' strike of 1842 as a, 'golden opportunity',

> the golden opportunity now within our grasp shall not pass away fruitless ... we do now universally resolve never to resume labour, until labour's grievances are destroyed ... Englishmen! The blood of your brethren reddens the streets of Preston and Blackburn.[149]

Workers and military had clashed at Preston and Blackburn with fatal results. As events were to unfold, the name of Halifax was quickly added to Preston and Blackburn's, in reprints of this statement and in reality. But for the time being all was relatively calm at Halifax; the strikers would not reach there for some days yet, although people were looking out for them from the direction of Hebden Bridge.

In the midst of all the excitement at Manchester, leaders of the nation's trades met there on 15th August, at the Sherwood Inn on Tib Street. There were representatives from the Wheelwrights and Blacksmiths' Society, the calico printers, hammermen, bootmakers, plumbers and glaziers, from hatters, cordwainers, joiners, painters, tailors, mechanics and more; there were representatives from the sawyers, plasterers, cotton spinners and hand-loom weavers, from factory operatives, moulders and boilermakers. The colliers sent representatives from Eccles, Oldham, Hopwood, and from Clayton came representatives Richard Rogers and William Wood.[150] At midday, the Sherwood Inn proving too small, these trade representatives moved to Carpenters' Hall before which 'two troops of the first Dragoons, two companies of the Grenadier Guards, a company of the 60th Rifles and a company of the 58th Regiment' were positioned.[151]

The presence of troops did not discourage a great crowd from gathering outside the hall. Everyone waited, eager to hear the decision made within. Inside, Alexander Hutchinson, delegate from the smiths, chaired proceedings and said their purpose was to come to a decision which many were waiting for, that they must 'prevent their fellow workmen from proceeding to their employment until they came to some conclusion; and ... it was necessary that they should provide for those now standing out. It was of importance', Hutchinson said, 'that they should carry everything out by moral force'.[152] Peaceably.

The Anti-Corn Law League 'hailed these disturbances as the first outbreak of the long prognosticated social revolution', the *Halifax Guardian* reported.[153] Interestingly, it was the Operative Anti-Corn-Law Association which, it is said, encouraged this conference hoping the delegates would decide to support the League's policies as a resolution to their problems.[154] After some hours, the trades' meeting produced the opposite of this. William Duffy, from the tailors, pointed out that Anti-Corn Law lecturers were 'at this moment, carrying staves as special constables',

> If these men think that they will intimidate us – that now, after having conjured up the public mind to the highest possible pitch, they can ... turn round and say, 'we are corn law leaguers to-day, and, *presto*, we are magistrates tomorrow ... they [are] much mistaken.[155]

The next day, the trades' delegates met at the Owenite Hall of Science. This time the authorities intervened. The meeting resolved, within the ten minutes it had left before the magistrates had everyone dispersed, to support the political aims of the Chartists. By now all the mill chimneys at Manchester were smokeless.

On that first day of the trades' meeting at Manchester, 15th August

1842, the multitude of turn-outs, already sweeping across the Pennines and gathering men and women to it from Rochdale and Todmorden, and from Hebden Bridge on the Yorkshire side, was drawing closer and closer to Halifax. Those who went into Huddersfield were described by the magistrates there as 'evidently in humble life – sensible, shrewd, determined, peaceable ... the burden of their speeches was to destroy no property, to hurt no human being, but determinedly to persist in ceasing from labour and to induce others to do the same until every man could obtain "a fair day's wage for a fair day's work"'.[156] The religiousness of so many of these men and women is an important underlying influence, their adherence to Methodism and Primitive Methodism brought huge discipline. And pledges of abstinence from alcohol had been made by many. These people, under duress, sought to behave in decent manner. But despite this general temperance, great disturbance and worse would take place at Halifax and Huddersfield, and across the whole of the industrialised West Riding, over the next forty-eight hours.

At Halifax, the first thing to happen, on news that the strikers were at last definitely approaching, was a movement, at dawn on 15th August, towards Skircoat Moor by those who had been waiting. The Moor lies only a mile from the town's centre. Crossley's Orphanage was not yet built, none of the houses now standing were built, so it extended much farther than today. 'The scenery viewed from the high ridge on the moor is both beautiful and romantic', wrote one contemporary observer of the southern aspect; another that it had 'no styles, no hedges or ditches – no narrow foot paths ... all is perfect and unrestrained freedom'.[157] On this high, open expanse, at break of day on Monday, 15th August, 1842, an excited crowd of people congregated to meet the marchers from Lancashire. They believed their time had come. They believed this was the dawn of change. Benjamin Rushton covered the three or four miles from Ovenden to be there, his purpose would be to keep the crowd focused and disciplined.

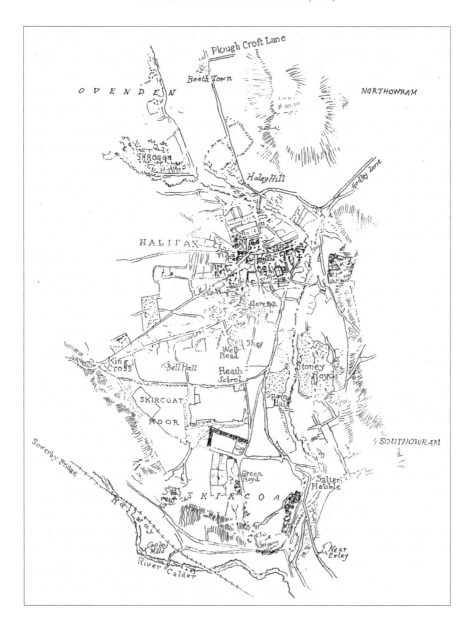

Already at Halifax there were one hundred and fifty of the 61st Regiment of Foot barracked near the Parish Church, and more than two hundred special constables had been sworn in the day before. Also, on this day, two troops of the 11th Hussars entered the town. Both troops, with their metal accoutrements glittering, would have looked impressive as they rode into the town. Two of Halifax's most effective magistrates, John

Rhodes Ralph and John Rawson were away at London, and the town was left with magistrates Mr. Waterhouse, Mr. Pollard and Mr. Briggs. John Waterhouse had grown too old to be sufficiently active, so responsibility for the whole defence of the town fell upon the last two men. After George Pollard's unsuccessful appeal to the crowd on Skircoat Moor to disperse and go back to their homes, Benjamin Rushton's speech was finally stopped by a police officer and, according to the *Halifax Guardian* reporter, the huge crowd dispersed 'like ice in hot water'. In fact, they all moved up to King Cross then on towards Luddenden Foot, in the direction from which the Lancashire marchers were coming.

One who saw the Lancashire marchers coming towards Halifax from Todmorden well remembers the crowd, 'coming along the turnpike after it had left Hebden Bridge',

> it was a remarkably fine day; the sun shone in its full splendour. The broad white road with its green hedges, and flanked one side with high trees, was filled with a long, black, straggling line of people, who cheerfully went along, evidently possessed of an idea that they were doing something towards a betterment. A number of us boys had been sent down into the woods to gather blackberries, and the woods were then clad in deep green; blackberries were plentiful, now they do not grow to maturity because of the smoke. The people went along over Fallingroyd Bridge towards Hawksclough. On reaching there, a local leader of the Chartist movement, Ben Rushton, stepped aside into a field, and led off with a speech. A number of those who were among the mass of the strikers, in going on their way, left the procession, went into the dwellings and helped themselves to whatever they could find in the way of food. Ben Rushton, I believe, was not one of these, nor were those that were with him. However, they were weary and thirsty, and before the speaking, a big milk can was obtained and filled with treacle beer, only the liquor had not been charged with yeast, nor had it had time to get fresh and tart. After the speaking the procession re-started and went on as before, and on to Halifax ...[158]

To add to their nightmare, the remaining Halifax magistrates learned from their Bradford colleagues early that morning, that as many marchers as were heading towards Halifax from Lancashire were heading towards Halifax, over the hills, from Bradford and the north-east. The Bradford workers had decided, that morning, to join their Halifax colleagues in welcoming the Lancashire marchers. The Bradford authorities' early warning of this march was accompanied with a troop of the 17th Lancers.

To the far side of Bradford, at Pudsey, one eye witness to events there wrote:

> I saw the plug drawers at Bankhouse and Fulneck, etc. The rioters marched there led by a man of the name of North, who lived in the neighbourhood of Bradford and was well known since that time in the same locality as a political reformer ... this man North stood up and addressed them, telling them that all his men had resolved to shed no blood except in self-defence, but had determined that no more work should be done till the "People's Charter" was the law of the land. He bared his breast as he spoke, and told both magistrates and soldiers, they might pierce his heart with bullets or lances, but the people were resolved to no longer starve when there was an abundance in the land, kept from the producers of all wealth by bad and unjust laws ... I saw North stand on an iron pipe in Claughton Garth Mill dam, and heard him tell his followers not to let it off, for in a few days they expected getting all they wanted, and to let off the dam would prevent the people from working for a long time to come. North at that day was a fine looking person, had a good address, was bold and self-possessed, had a clear and distinct expression, was very fluent in speech, and just the man to fill his followers with confidence.[159]

Nothing can tell more eloquently the feeling of working people that day, that they believed they were coming in on the tide of a great political change. At Halifax, the Lancashire marchers had arrived at King Cross, to the west of the town. These many thousands were lead by women, walking four abreast, just as they had at Manchester, and all were singing Chartist hymns, and delivering in song Psalm 100:

> Shout with joy to the Lord, O earth
> Worship the Lord with gladness
> Come before him, singing with joy,

Acknowledge that the Lord is God.

He made us, and we are his.

We are his people, the sheep of his pasture

Enter his gates with thanksgiving,

Go into his courts with praise.

Give thanks to him and bless his name.

For the Lord is good.

His unfailing love continues forever,

And his faithfulness continues to each generation.

They crossed the town's boundaries unchallenged because Major Burnside, of the 61st Regiment of Foot, Captain Forrest's Hussars and all the two hundred or so special constables were gathered at the Piece Hall. It was decided at the Piece Hall that all should be actively deployed at the northern side of the town at New Bank, the road running up from North Bridge to Shibden, mainly to protect the two large mills there, Akroyd's and Haigh's, and stop the Bradford marchers entering the town. So, astonishingly, the Lancashire marchers came on unhindered, they and their Yorkshire hosts, all together from the other side of the town. Now all gets difficult and confused. Some unidentified person, on horseback, directed the Lancashire men and women's attention to the mills to be visited and disabled. The bulk of the crowd moved on, down, towards the town's centre, in the direction from which the strikers from Bradford were coming.

At the same time, the first of the Bradford men and women appeared at the top of New Bank. The whole of Halifax town was spread out before them in bright daylight, and down the road, immediately below them and blocking the way, was the troop of the 17th Lancers. At this very moment, Major Burnside's and Captain Forrest's men, with the large contingent of special constables and magistrates William Briggs and George Pollard, were gathering at the foot of New Bank. The sight of the marchers, emerging above them from the shade of Godley Cutting and out onto the crest of the road, would be something not quickly forgotten. They came, old and young, men and women, all visibly destitute and emotionally excited, many carrying some kind of weapon.

Skircoat Green teenager, Benjamin Wilson, was naturally active throughout all of this. On hearing of the approaching marchers from Bradford he made his way to Halifax 'as fast as possible', and met them at the top of New Bank.

> I was much surprised when I saw thousands of men and women marching in procession, many of whom were armed with cudgels. I then marched down New Bank with them, but we had not got far before we saw a great number of special constables, and soldiers with bayonets fixed and swords drawn coming out of the town. We met them a little above Berry's Foundry and there they stopped us; they were accompanied by some of the magistrates ...[160]

The magistrates came forward. George Pollard asked the marchers to turn back and go home. The crowd, with Radical green flags flying, did not budge. There were calls of 'Go on, go on'. George Pollard read the Riot Act and, for the benefit of anyone too far up the road to hear, placards stating that the Riot Act had been read were raised into the air from within the ranks of the special constables. The number of marchers able to decipher the markings on the placards would be minimal. Confronted by such a large military presence and, 'seeing the impossibility of forcing our way through them', Benjamin Wilson said, 'we made our way over the walls and through the fields, which were not built upon at that time, and came down Range Bank to Northgate'.

And so the Lancashire marchers and the Bradford marchers surged forward into Halifax. These two great crowds of people met on Crown Street, in the town's centre, and merged from there down to the North Bridge. The strangeness of it, and the excitement must have been euphoric. 'The streets became blocked, and it was said there were 25,000 women and men there'. At this point some were still singing. A hymn to the tune of the 'Old Hundred', and another to a tune called 'Lydia' were heard. 'They were poorly clad, and many were without shoes and stockings, barefooted'.[161] Sympathisers, perhaps appeasers also, left bread and bowls of fresh water and mugs for them on their doorsteps.

Then the swell turned back on itself, towards North Bridge and

Akroyd's and Haighs' mills and towards the oncoming body of soldiers which was stoned by at least one young boy, Benjamin Wilson, from the advantage point of Red Tom's field, close by North Parade, and which was elevated some twelve feet above road level. On Park Street, the bulk of the crowd, still led by its women, came face-to-face with the soldiers. Disorder swelled, the Riot Act was read again, the placards raised again, but this time the crowd laughed. The women came right up to the 'very necks' of the soldiers' horses, saying they would 'die rather than starve', and that if the soldiers were determined to charge, then let them come and kill them. This was a pivotal moment and there were clear tactics at use here. The women would know that the soldiers were less likely to attack them than they were to attack the men. Also, while this enormous crowd of people was engaging the attention of the soldiers and special constables in the streets of Halifax, small groups of efficient men were entering the town's mills, knocking in the boiler plugs and letting off the steam. There was some danger of scalding in this operation. The *Halifax Guardian* told its readers how successful these men were in disabling the mills at Halifax that day, 'so quietly and systematically did they proceed about their work that we believe in no single instance did they encounter either the military or the police'.[162] From the bottom of Salterhebble Hill right across to Akroyd's mill below Boothtown, everything was stopped within a matter of hours. And, overlooking the whole event in clear, bright sunshine, a small committee of turnouts remained the entire time at the top of New Bank, their purpose being to release messenger pigeons, perhaps to a central authority back in Lancashire, perhaps to closer destinations but certainly with the intention of keeping absent but interested parties informed of events at Halifax as they unfolded.

Down in Halifax town, Captain Forrest was ordered to clear the streets around North Parade. His men of the Hussars, 'formed in a close and compact line, and moved slowly forward; the toes of the front ranks in the mob must have been most severely crushed', the *Guardian*'s reporter wrote. The process of clearing the streets was not really such an orderly process. 'Many people were trampled under the horses' feet, and many people were injured', said one eye-witness.[163] Bayonets were used, but none pressed home. William Southwell from Mytholmroyd, who was marked out as a leader, was arrested and there were more arrests at Northgate and North Bridge by the 61st of Foot. An isolated contingent of soldiers actually fired on a group of turn-outs when an attempt was made by them to rescue prisoners being taken to the lock-up. One worker was injured in his leg.[164]

The special constables also were, 'vigorous in their attacks upon the mob, hundreds of whom they disarmed of their bludgeons', one Halifax reporter stated.[165] At last Captain Forrest's Hussars galloped through the town scattering any still there. By two o'clock that afternoon the marchers and their hosts had retreated and assembled on Skircoat Moor in their tens of thousands. '[W]hen I arrived' says Benjamin Wilson, 'I saw such a sight as I had never seen there before, the moor being literally covered with men and women, the bulk of them sat down getting something to eat which had been given them on their way'.[166]

On Skirocat Moor more speeches were made, a deputation was sent to ask for the release of the prisoners taken by the soldiers and police that day, and John Whiteley from Skircoat Green offered up a prayer on behalf of everyone there. And there everyone remained, for the rest of that day and night.

The crowd which had come from Bradford walked the miles back home that same evening. An eye witness remembers seeing them, when he was a boy of ten, as they came down from Queensbury and through Horton towards the city. 'The sight' he says' was just one of those which it is impossible to forget ...'

> They came pouring down the wide road in thousands, taking up its whole breadth – a gaunt, famished-looking, desperate multitude armed with huge bludgeons, flails, pitchforks and pikes, many without coats and hats, and hundreds upon hundreds with their clothes in rags and tatters. Many of the older men looked footsore and weary, but the great bulk were men in the prime of life, full of wild excitement. As they marched they thundered out to a grand old tune a stirring melody, of which this was the opening stanza : –

"Men of England, ye are slaves,
Though ye "rule" the roaring "waves,"
Though ye shout, 'From sea to sea
Britons everywhere are free'"

As the wild mob swept onward, terrified women brought out all their bread and other eatables, and in the hope of purchasing their forbearance, handed them to the rough-looking men who crowded to the doors and windows. A famished wretch, after struggling feebly for a share of the provisions, fell down in a fainting condition in the doorway where I was standing. A doctor, who lived close at hand, was got to the spot as soon as possible, but the man died in his presence. One of his comrades told us that the poor fellow had eaten raw potatoes at Ovenden after being without food two days; these the doctor said had killed him, "raw potatoes on an empty stomach being poison".[167]

Benjamin Rushton had been a significant presence throughout all of this day. He had walked miles and miles and had spoken tirelessly all that day too, to thousands of people, carrying with him the knowledge that his wife, Mary, was very ill at home. He leaves the image of a quiet pillar of a man. His twenty-year-old near-neighbour, John Snowden, was one of those arrested on Monday 15th August. He got caught up in the action at Haley Hill and Boothtown. This is how it happened.

Although the Halifax authorities had been so concerned to save Haigh's and Akroyd's mills when the marchers first arrived at Halifax, to the point of leaving open entry into the town to the thousands of Lancashire marchers, both mills were stopped by the turn-outs while the soldiers and specials were kept busy by the crowd in the town's centre. Haighs' was stopped by John Hodgson who, coming face-to-face with one of Mr. Haigh's sons as he drove in the plugs, said none would be satisfied until the Charter was won. The second, Mr. Akroyd's, was stopped by a weaver named William Jackson Cockroft. William Jackson Cockroft approached the mill at the Shade with other men and found Jonathan Akroyd there. Akroyd managed to prevent any but one of their party entering and so, while his colleagues waited outside, William Cockroft went in alone to pull the plugs. It was Akroyd's own engineer, at his employer's request, who did the job when Cockroft's efforts failed, then Jonathan Akroyd, it is said, gave the turn-outs four guineas with the request that they spend it on bread for their women.[*]

While this was going on at the Akroyd mill, the rest of the turn-outs proceeded on, up the hill, to Boothtown while others turned into Jonathan Akroyd's grounds at Woodside intent on letting off the reservoir there. It was here that John Snowden ran into trouble although he always maintained he had been with this group of men only as an observer. He was with this latter party when it found the Akroyd grounds faithfully defended by armed men. And then, when numbers of Hussars galloped into the grounds all was lost and six of the trespassers were arrested, one being John Snowden.

Meanwhile, the remainder of this party of turn-outs, led by a weaver from Wheatley called Thomas Barker, had arrived at Boothtown a short distance higher up the hill. This group of strikers brought out Atkinson's silk workers and then they somehow succeeded in stopping the work of Joseph Stock's miners at Boothtown Colliery. Patience Kershaw, even if she was half-a-mile underground for most of it, would know of this disturbance at her place of work and wonder at its meaning.

Later in the day, reporters from the *Halifax Guardian* mingled with the great crowd of people who had retired to Skircoat Moor. In all likelihood the leading reporter of the day was Henry French Etherington, a man not much in sympathy with the workers' cause.[§] As the evening drew on, he and his colleagues overheard conversations between the campers who stretched themselves out in circular groups across the Moor

---

[*] If this tale is in fact a true one, Jonathan Ackyroyd's behaviour is interesting. He was a man opposed to industrial reform and who cut his workers' wages with very little compunction. He was also a non-Conformist Christian who would have believed in the idea of the sacrificial lamb. Expressions of self-sacrifice would have had deep meaning to him. Driving in his own boiler plugs and giving large sums of money to his attackers tallies with notions of Christian self-sacrifice as a way to bring forth good from bad and could have been an expression of his belief in himself as a man of God.

[§] The *Halifax Guardian* was published from the Black Swan Passage off George Street. Its first editor was George Hogarth, Charles Dickens' future father-in-law, who by this time had been replaced by E. J. Walker.

and heard the Chartist hymns these people sang. There were many women there the reporters noted, and they said a number of these women were urging the men on with talk of what should be done about their compatriots taken that day: "Ye're soft if ye don't fetch 'em out to neet". [168] Like Eve, they are said to be tempting their men to action. The next day's events were, perhaps, being prescribed. One thing is certain, whether or not the women's incitement accounted for the next day's events, for some those events would be terrible.

11

The Salterhebble Hill Attack (1842)

Blows had been struck against the 'white slavery', the 'factory slavery', the 'Yorkshire slavery' of the industrialists, against all that those terms meant to the strikers. The great strike had been going on for almost a week in other parts, and now, at Halifax too, everything was at a standstill. On this same day, Monday 15th, the Home Secretary, Sir James Graham, wrote to the Northern Military Commander, Major General Warre, urging him to arrest the trades' leaders at Manchester and, soon after, he wrote to the Queen assuring her that the country's property owners had begun to defend themselves, 'against these bands of plunderers, who are the enemies both of law and order and of property'.[169] James Graham would be acutely aware that it was impossible to defend against a determined populace, 'even if', he wrote, 'you had a standing army ten times greater than the British to provide troops for every town and village throughout the manufacturing districts'. The knowledge that London showed no sign of rising would be of great comfort to him. Unlike Paris less than fifty years before, in London there would be no storming of Bastilles and no guillotines.

At Halifax, a great many of the visiting turn-outs prepared to move off the next morning, Tuesday 16th August. How did these people feel, the majority? Hopeful and 'excited', 'determined' and, according to Henry French Etherington and his fellow reporters, ready to listen to addresses given by speakers, 'most temperate in their language'. These speakers, according to the *Halifax Guardian*, 'pretended to dissuade the meeting from all acts of violence', one advising those who heard him, 'not even to pluck an ear of wheat without the owner's leave'.[170]

The meeting that morning on Skircoat Moor heard prayers then speeches. One speaker from Bradford recommended a concentration of their efforts at Halifax because here great attempts would be made to put the people down: 'if Halifax is lost, all will be lost'. Of the region's mill owners, few were as influential as those at Halifax and the most influential of these were known to be effective opposers to factory reform.

On this morning of 16th August 1842, many of the visitors left the Moor. Sunrise would have been at about six o'clock and the marchers would, very likely, have moved off an hour or two after this; after the speeches. Passing close by Skircoat Green, they made their way down the steep, twisting roadway known as Salterhebble Hill to the canal docks and on to Elland through Greetland. The mills along the way were stopped as they passed through a perfect summer's morning. Then the atmosphere seemed to change. A great many of those remaining were not feeling as peaceable as early reports suggest. They knew that yesterday's prisoners would be escorted to Elland railway station during the morning, to be put onto the Wakefield train. In the minds of those remaining at Halifax were the bayonet 'pricks', the broken bones and the soldiers' rifle shots of yesterday.

There was a visitor to the town at this time, an engineer by profession, who was working on the construction of the branch line to connect Halifax to the Manchester-Leeds rail. His name was Francis Grundy.[171] The day before, when the Lancashire marchers had first arrived at Halifax, he had been tucked away with friends, in pleasant ignorance of what was going on in the town. His ignorance was not to last. Francis Grundy's office happened to be at the foot of Salterhebble Hill, close beneath the 'short lanes or alleys, which sloped upwards towards the summit of the hills to either side, and commanded … a considerable stretch of the highway'. As he made his way there, on the morning of Tuesday 16th August, he was 'quite amazed at the number of people who were hurrying in the same direction'. 'The route was like a road to a fair or to the races. All were going the same way'.[172] But he noticed something else; that some were gathering into a large crowd just across from his office, and that there were:

> women as well as men … rushing along the various lanes over my head
> with arms and aprons full of stones, taken from the macadamized heaps
> of blue metal placed along the turnpike road.[173]

The woods still stand above the road from Halifax to Elland through which these lanes run and to where these women and men were fetching stones.

At midday, 'Suddenly' said Grundy, 'all was still'.

Then, a whistle came from the heights soon followed by the sound of horses and vehicles coming along the road from Halifax town. Two omnibuses appeared at the top of Salterhebble Hill escorted by '8 Soldiers, a Sergeant, a Corporal & Lieut. W.G. Pitt', and the magistrate William Briggs and his groom.[174] These were the omnibuses carrying to Elland railway station the prisoners arrested the day before and which included John Snowden. 'Down they rattle with all the pride and pomp of a crack regiment', said Francis Grundy, and, 'Bravo! … the conspirators are not ready'. It seems the crowd was not yet organised. It met the procession at the bottom of Salterhebble Hill. The omnibuses passed and some stones were thrown at the soldiers who passed unscathed and they and their prisoners went on to Elland. Everyone assumed the soldiers would be returning along the same way.

'My windows and small balcony command the winding stretch of road over which the hussars must come back again', wrote Francis Grundy. 'The gathering multitude increases momentarily, the collecting of stones goes on unceasingly'.

> Where the road crosses the canal, two hundred yards away, a bridle-path leads down to the towing-path. Here the canal turns suddenly to the right, skirting the hill, and … opposite the ambush, there is a steep slope forty or fifty feet high, and a flat lowland one hundred yards across, between it and the hill. I see that if I can only meet the returning troops and show this by-path to them, they may escape. How to reach them is the question. I must try it![175]

He decided he must meet the troops out of sight of the waiting crowd by going some way to meet them, and he must not create suspicion. He feigned nonchalance. He leant out of his window and smoked 'indifferently' as he chatted to his men who were 'idling around'. Then he made his way outside and smoked some more, leaning against the rail. '[T]hen I go quietly and slowly down the steps into the road, and stand there, still talking to my men about the works'. Under the pretended purpose of checking progress of work on the foundations to the bridge they were building he began to make his way down the road in the direction of Elland. He went a few dozen yards when two heavy hands fell upon his shoulders. They were the hands of two of his own men.

"Thou mustn't go t'ut brigg to-day, sir', one said. Grundy objected. "We be main sorry, sir … but thou mun come back again … Thou'lt nobbut be murdered, and thou cannot do ony guid. There are a matter of fower [four] thousand folk looking on; so come, sir. Thou'rt not to be fettled, but thou'rt to be kept insoide o' t'house".[176] Grundy had to return to his office with his men, to watch what would unfold.

As chance would have it, the first vehicle to arrive at Salterhebble from Elland was not one of the prisoners' omnibuses, which were left behind at Elland by the soldiers, but a private vehicle carrying eight passengers to Halifax who had alighted from an incoming Leeds train. One of these passengers was a reporter from the *Northern Star* come to investigate what had happened the day before. As it entered the turnpike road running through Elland Woods, a crowd of people along that part of the road moved in on the vehicle from the trees and started throwing stones at it as it made its way along. They thought it was the soldiers' vehicle. The omnibus driver controlled his horses sufficiently to get his vehicle through this danger before being confronted with the greater one at Salterhebble Hill. The Salterhebble crowd also thought his was one of the prisoners' omnibuses returning with officials and he was compelled to draw up. The horses' heads were seized.

> Women, armed with tremendous bludgeons, were more violent even than
> the men, and the omnibus and its passengers seemed threatened with
> instant destruction.[177]

Some talk took place between the assailants and the travellers until the crowd eventually realized that this vehicle had nothing to do with the soldiers and it was allowed to continue on up the hill. 'It's not you we want, it's the magistrates and soldiers', one woman was overheard to say. Safe passage was given, and the vehicle began, slowly, chaperoned by one of the crowd, to climb the hill. At which point, the magistrate and soldiers emerged from Exley Bank, at the bottom of the hill.

Earlier, at Elland, the soldiers and William Briggs had arrived only just in time to get their prisoners safely into the departing train, then Mr. Briggs had directed the soldiers to take the higher road through Exley for their return journey to Halifax, thinking to avoid a confrontation with the crowd in Elland Wood down below. They might have avoided the majority of the multitude at Salterhebble too, by continuing along the Southowram hillside, but, strangely, they did not. Now, at sight of them coming out onto the road at the foot of Salterhebble Hill, a cry went up in the crowd and 'suddenly the appearance of calm was succeeded with an overwhelming tempest, for in an instant, as it were, a shower of large stones were hurled from all parts of the eminence among the soldiers'.[178] The eight soldiers of the 11th Hussars, 'their accoutrements glittering in the sunshine', spurred their horses on to overtake Mr. Briggs who had been leading on his horse in company with his groom, but not before the magistrate's mount was hit on its head by a stone. The Hussars gallop forward but at reaching the base of Salterhebble Hill,

> Great stones, hurled by a thousand strong hands, jostle and split, diverging upon that small space where ride the lancers in all the pomp of military pride. 'Gallop! gallop!' comes the order, as their leader spurs his horse up the steep hill.[179]

The private vehicle and its passengers were caught up in this assault part way up the hill and the coach driver was 'unable to command his horses'. His leader shyed and the soldiers coming up at the time became 'entangled with the omnibus horses'.[180] The *Northern Star* reporter, sitting up on the box with the driver, as well as a young woman who sat between them, both were hit on the head by flying stones, another about his legs. But the soldiers on the hill had by far the worst of it. It is reckoned on the day that these stones each weighed between five and twenty pounds. Under this hail of stones five of the soldiers' horses, 'close by the wells', went down, throwing their riders, 'three being underneath their animals'.[181] From his office window, Francis Grundy watched on:

> horsemen, bleeding and helpless, crawled about the road seeking shelter. Some lay still as death. Now and again a horse struggled to rise, and with shrill scream fell back upon the ground. A man or horse once or twice, less hurt than their fellows, limped slowly away.

All reports agree that three of the Hussars were left behind, and once the main body of the soldiery, which fired at the crowd as it retreated, had reached the top of the hill ...

> Down came the hosts now, and tearing the belts and accoutrements from the prostrate hussars, the saddles and bridles from their horses, they give three cheers ...[182]

Some began to beat and kick the downed soldiers while others tried to stop them. The soldiers who had made it to the top of the hill rallied, then they saw their fellow troop of Hussars, which all this time had remained at

Halifax, coming along the road towards them, to see how things were going. They sent back for all the military still at Halifax to reinforce their numbers. Then, without waiting longer, they made a counter attack. Eyewitness, France Grundy, says the soldiers came 'swooping down at a run, with bayonets fixed'. His recollection is that foot soldiers as well as men of the 11th Hussars were there.[183] William Briggs, the magistrate, went down the hill with them. In fact, it was said he led them. He was struck by a large coping stone which broke his arm. The soldiers used their firearms and there was intimation, in newspaper reports, that one of the crowd was hit and killed. However, the soldiers' retaliation 'was useless', said Francis Grundy, who watched the crowd scattering, melting away into the hillsides; 'there was no enemy' for the soldiers to engage.

The three felled soldiers were retrieved, and they and their rescuers returned to the toll bar at the top of Salterhebble Hill, by Dry Clough Junction. Two had been found at the house of one Mr. Lees, the third in a house near the quarry. Their names were Alexander Fraser, John Austin and Thomas Clarkson and all were treated at the Northgate Hotel by the surgeon, Mr. Garlick. John Austin 'was the most severely injured of the three, having his right eye completely blocked up, and being most severely beaten and kicked about his legs and body. Fraser also was barbarously dealt with and it was only through the merciful interference of a portion of their assailants that their lives were not sacrificed'.[184] Mr. Garlick did not shrink from presenting his bill. Regimental records show zero payments to private medical practitioners in 1842 with the exception of July-Sept when the Paymaster met bills of £13.14.6.[185] Benjamin Wilson was later to repeat hearsay that one of the three captured soldiers had 'begged for his life', and had died from his wounds.[186] There is no evidence of military deaths and the fact is that all three soldiers downed that day were safely back at their Barnsley barracks by the end of the year.[187]

The omnibus made it to the top of the hill at about the same time as the body of soldiers, its windows smashed, its body dented, its horses distressed, one of them injured, and its passengers injured or shaken. Benjamin Wilson, who had come down from Skircoat Green to watch proceedings, said he saw the injured magistrate, William Briggs, coming up with it. James Holroyd, the Halifax surgeon, was called to attend to the passenger with the leg injuries.

After the riots of the day before, all military personnel had made their joint headquarters in the yard and stables at the back of the Northgate Hotel and when the summons for every available man from the commander at Salterhebble reached there and the infantry began its rushed way through the town to join the assaulted troops, along with some two hundred of the special constables lead by magistrate George Pollard, the town was in an instant stir wondering what could be happening now. Halfway there, the omnibus, now making its way towards Halifax in the company of the entire contingent of Hussars, met them on their way out. Young Benjamin Wilson was one of those following the omnibus towards the town and heard an officer tell the oncoming troops and specials that the crowd at Salterhebble was numbered in the thousands and that there was no use in going back. The combined forces of the two troops of Hussars and the two companies of the 61st Regiment of Foot amounted to a maximum of two hundred and fifty men. They returned together to Halifax. The Hussars were deeply humiliated. The treatment they had received, 'appeared to have enraged them', Benjamin thought.

Newtown apart, Salterhebble was the one incident during all these years when a town's inhabitants set out deliberately to attack a troop of soldiers. Francis Grundy was left with the impression, uncorroborated, that, '[o]ne man, said to be *the* crack man of his crack regiment, lay dead under his dead horse; another died in a few minutes; and I believe that several were long in hospital ...'. His ominous judgement, this time horribly accurate, of that morning's work was that the troops returning to Halifax were, 'more infuriated than ever ... But the mob was wild too; it had tasted blood, and was thirsting for more slaughter'.[188]

Meanwhile at the Northgate Hotel, the troops having returned and gone out again onto the streets, someone sat down to write a report destined for the magistrates at Leeds. The writer did not give his name. It was mid-afternoon as he began to write:

A most terrible affair has occurred at Salter Hebble and at the time I write it is feared there will be many lives lost before the day is over – I scarcely know how to inform you in a few lines the dreadful state of things in Halifax and the neighbourhood – the Town presents an awful state of things – the Turn outs are crowding all the streets and have been going about all the morning ... I have seen the wounded soldiers and they are really dreadfully beaten. The Mob kicked them when down ... The Military are all out – the special constables also – The Mob are at Skircoat Moor and it is said here at the Northgate Hotel that they are expected down shortly, when the Military will I am positively assured receive instructions to fire upon them ... Mr Akroyd (I have seen him) is quite overwhelmed in difficulties – the Mob keep him at Bay and he has his premises completely barricaded - the Soldiers wounded are of the 11th Hussars, from Barnsley which came in here last night and the Soldiers swear they will have their Revenge.[189]

At four that afternoon, the great crowd did come down, into the town, and the soldiers did have their revenge.

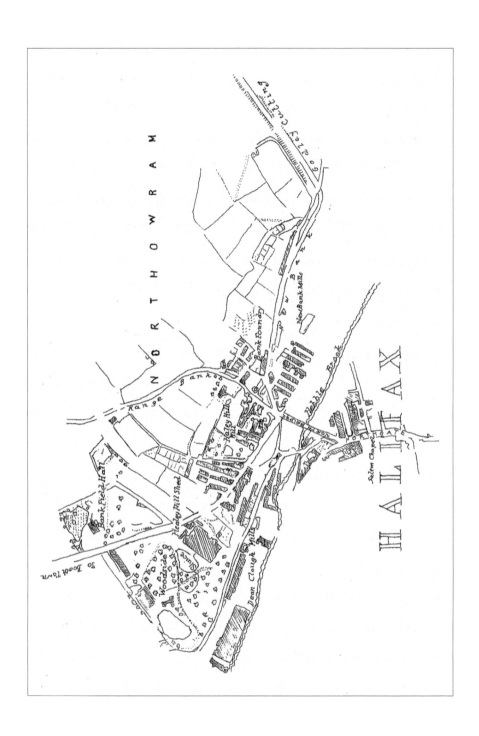

12

The Haley Hill Attack (1842)

On the morning of the Salterhebble battle, Tuesday 16th August, Halifax received a Royal Proclamation from London which read:

BY THE QUEEN – A PROCLAMATION

Whereas in divers part of Great Britain, great multitudes of lawless and disorderly persons have lately assembled themselves together in a riotous and tumultuous manner, and have, by threats and intimidation, prevented our good subjects therein employed from following their usual occupations and earning their livelihood. We, therefore, being duly sensible of the mischievous consequences which must inevitably ensue, as well to the peace of the kingdom, as to the lives and properties of our subjects, from such wicked and illegal practices, if they go unpunished … we do hereby promise and declare, that any person or persons who shall discover and apprehend, the authors, abettors, or perpetrators of any of the outrages above mentioned, so that they, or any of them, may be duly convicted thereof, shall be entitled to the sum of £50 for each and every person whom shall be convicted, and shall also receive our most gracious pardon for the said offence, in case the person making such discovery as aforesaid shall be liable to be prosecuted for the same. Given at our court at Windsor …[190]*

This was quickly posted up in the streets of Halifax, together with the magistrates' own placard which read:

All strangers and other persons are hereby required to depart to their homes instantly, as the Magistrates are determine that the Military shall clear the streets be the consequence what it may.

Everything was pointing towards disaster. A proud, glittering platoon of the 11th Hussars, Prince Albert's Own, had been unhorsed and blooded; it was assumed at the Northgate Hotel that the soldiers would, before the day was

---

* At that time it would take a woolcomber, weaver, mill or mine worker about two years' work to earn £50

out, receive the order to fire at the crowd and there was open talk of revenge among them. The magistrates' placard was a green light to the soldiers and the local turn-outs did not intend to turn around and go home. Express appeals were sent from Halifax to Bradford and Leeds, 'for a further support of the military', but neither town was able to spare troops.[191]

After the stoning at Salterhebble, the crowd had made its way back to Skircoat Moor. There it was resolved that everyone should go to Haley Hill, to the place of the great Akroyd, Haigh and Crossley mills, and at mid-afternoon they made their way into Halifax. After the affrays of the day before, 'business seemed to be at a standstill in the town and neighbourhood', recalled Benjamin Wilson. The mills of the Akroyd and Haigh families, Crossley's Dean Clough mills, Atkinson's silk mill, Dawson's mill, everything was stopped. Shops and beer-houses were closed.

The magistrate, William Briggs, disappeared from the scene at this point. His arm was broken, he had participated, boldly, in a military skirmish and he retired to his home and his bed. The last remaining active magistrate, George Pollard, waited at the Northgate Hotel.

Francis Grundy, notwithstanding his sentiments which harmonise with the authorities, described how a crowd appeared in front of the Northgate Hotel and the special constables were first sent out to face them. He said stones were thrown. The Riot Act was read. Then, from the rear yard came numbers of the 61st of Foot, which Grundy refers to as the 60th, and behind them the Hussars. The special constables, he said, turned and went back to the hotel's yard leaving the infantry facing the crowd. The soldiers prepared, fired over the people's heads and then the order was given to fire at them: 'fire *low* this time!'. The crowd was hit, there was panic and people ran in every available direction while the Hussars came out from behind the infantry, 'and the charging horsemen ... dashed amongst the mixed multitudes'.

> Many threw themselves down, when the horses, more merciful than their riders, leapt over them, while the hussars cut furiously at them with their sabres. They followed the flying people ... and returned revenged'.[192]

There is no corroboration of this event with the one exception of a newspaper report of an attack, on this day, upon John Holroyd, a Rishworth mill worker, who was bayoneted five times on Broad Street in the town's centre; twice in the thigh, once under his shoulder blade, once at his hip bone and again at the back of his ear. Official reports described his injuries as slight.[193] Matham Crook, a man from Boothtown, also was attacked, but not quite so badly injured. And there is the mention from the nameless writer at the Northgate Hotel that the troops were out on the streets at this time. John Holroyd, whose ordeal was corroborated in Home Office papers, would survive his injuries which were not as bad as those to be endured by others at Haley Hill, beyond the town's centre, before the day was out.

No explanation is given for the turn-outs' concentration on Akroyd's mill. Jonathan Akroyd had escaped relatively unscathed the day before, dealing with just the one intruder intent on disabling his works; his reservoir successfully defended. Now he was preparing for much worse. There were many workers' houses at Haley Hill. Patience Kershaw's sister Sybil lived there, and many bystanders from these houses had come out to watch what was happening. 'Every precaution had been taken for the preservation' of Akroyd's mill at the Shade, said the Halifax reporter,

[a] quantity of armed men were placed within the premises, and the entrance to the Shade was guarded by a powerful force; a number of men armed with staves were also in attendance. The Mill at Bowling Dyke was also equally well guarded. The large gates forming the principal entrance were barricaded with wool sacks piled against them. The only entrance being through a narrow gateway, and down a number of steps which were protected by a number of chains fixed in a zig-zag direction so as effectually to check any rush that might be made. At the top of a large warehouse adjoining the Shade a man was stationed to communicate by telegraph when the military would be required.[194]

At around four o'clock on the afternoon of 16th August 1842, about four hours after the events on Salterhebble Hill, the turn-outs began to arrive at Haley Hill, their numbers still being swelled by those coming across North Bridge. Akroyd's mill was indeed defended, very much more effectively than it had been the day before, by many of its workers who had been sworn in as special constables. The telegraph to which the Halifax reporter referred, was, in fact, a rigged-up system whereby the mill could alert the soldiers in the town that their assistance was needed by raising a flag through a hole which had been made in the mill's roof. Before the main body of the crowd had reached Haley Hill, a number of turn-outs managed to get into the mill, through the barricades, and they were very easily made prisoners there when the doors were locked behind them. The roof top flag was waved, it was seen by the lookout on the roof of the Northgate Hotel and the soldiers quickly began to make their way from the town centre, no more than half-a-mile away.

Hundreds of people were still crossing North Bridge towards Haley Hill as the Hussars began to make their way across it, at a hand gallop, the foot soldiers following on at a good jog through the crowd. The *Northern Star*'s reporter told his readers to remember that, at this time, 'there was no attack upon Akroyd's mill' ...

> the only symptoms of such an attack being contemplated by the people,
> was the entrance of the few stragglers, who were secure in the mill ...

It is now that the *Halifax Guardian* says a shot was fired from within the crowd, while the *Northern Star* reporter, backed-up by the *Leeds Mercury* reporter, made no mention of gun shots from the crowd. He said there were 'different statements' as to what happened, 'but all agree in this' he wrote,

> that there was no regular attack upon the mill, and that the people were
> not causing any further disturbance than must necessarily be caused by
> the passage of so large a multitude along the road.[195]

One man making his way over the bridge was 'pricked' by a foot soldier's bayonet when he got in his way, and was then struck down by the same soldier's rifle butt when he remonstrated. A stir began and then things escalated very quickly. Magistrates John Rhodes Ralph and John Rawson were still out of town, William Briggs was recuperating at home, and of the two remaining magistrates, George Pollard was the one in charge, supported by Bradford magistrate, L.W. Hird. Hird and the military were seen talking together, the order was given and the soldiers fired into the crowd. At first their fire was sporadic and then it became a regular volley. Now the Hussars, fresh from the morning's humiliation, came up into the crowd, attacking with their sabres. 'The people seemed terror-stricken', said the Halifax reporter. One man in the crowd, Henry Walton, from Skircoat Green, received an appalling sabre cut to the top of his head which he could not possibly survive. Another, Charles Taylor, received a cut to his face which would at best only severely disfigure him. Now at the Shade, the troops fired into the crowd again. Judging by reports, things grew more frenzied. William Sutcliffe's leg was smashed with a bullet below his knee rendering him unlikely ever to work as a delver again. The Hussars continued to cut people 'dreadfully' about their heads, their horses trampled on others. At a distance from the affray, a fifty-year-old stone mason called Jonathan Booth, who had come out to watch the event, somehow received a shot from behind which passed through his abdomen and out, through his front. A similar fate befell a young man called Sutton Briggs, standing 'at least 400 yards from the military upon the hillside', who was shot through the groin.[196] One of the mill-owning Crossley family was watching on from the same patch as Sutton Briggs.

At least one stone, or brick, was thrown on the soldiers from one of the worker's houses on Haley Hill. A soldier was hit and they ...

> rushed into what is known as 'the Square' in search of the miscreant, they broke open the doors and windows of one house and searched it, but found no one, as the occupants were gone into the country out of the way, as many others had done; ... in the next one searched they found two little girls in the cellar, and one of the special constables with the soldiers gave them a penny each; the next they entered was a widow's and one of her sons had just gone in, he was in his shirt sleeves, being a comber and working at his own home two doors off, he had a wife and two or three small children, and seizing him they pulled him out of the house but his wife declared if they took him they would have to take her and her child she had in her arms, she went down Haley Hill with them, and just before entering North Bridge he was released. This man was more fortunate than his next door neighbour who served a long term of imprisonment.[197]

Benjamin Wilson recalled hearing of this long after the event, when he had a chance to 'talk this matter over' with the man who had been imprisoned and who assured Benjamin he had been innocent.

The infantry, still firing at random into the crowd at Haley Hill, used up many rounds of ammunition. The *Halifax Guardian* reporter was surprised at the number and said the sound of the firing rifles was heard from a long way off. It certainly would reach Plough Croft Lane from Haley Hill with only a short sound delay, the two are so closely situated. And '[i]t created the most dire alarm through the town'.[198] Some of the crowd moved uphill towards Jonathan Akroyd's private premises, 'however they were met by a well-directed fire from the men in defence of the mansion', these being Akroyd's own men. Several men, 'were shot on the hillside, one man was wounded near the mill chimney'. The *Halifax Guardian* reporter said that firearms were used against the soldiers by the turn-outs in the Akroyd grounds.

The frenzy ended. Prisoners were taken and kept under guard until everything was over then they were taken to the police-house in the town. It was now, in the town centre, that the shooting of an elderly man called Samuel Crowther was witnessed by the two Leeds newspaper reporters. Samuel Crowther, a nail maker, was walking down a now almost empty King Street to his house, when a solitary soldier standing on the street raised his rifle at him. There was a moment's poise. Then the soldier fired. The hit man reeled at the impact before covering the final few feet, without making any sound, to his house. Within a moment or two, from the house came women shouting that he had been shot. The Leeds reporters entered the house and found Samuel Crowther bleeding and in terrible pain from a shot through his abdomen. He was taken to the infirmary. Officers of the soldier's regiment, upon investigation, found that stones had earlier been thrown in the street at the returning troop. They assumed the elderly nail maker, Samuel Crowther, had thrown them which seemed to justify his shooting.

There were now dozens of injured people making their way about the north side of Halifax. A number went to Mr. Wood, a chemist close by

Haley Hill, who dressed their wounds. One young man from Sowerby, after having his head-wound dressed, disappeared from Halifax.[199] The injured knew that to disappear was the only way to avoid the authorities. It seems that, out of all those injured, just four applied to the infirmary for help. Benjamin Wilson says one died on his way there. If so, this might have been Sutton Briggs, the young man who was shot while watching on. Another was the stonemason, Jonathan Booth who, soon after being shot, had been put into a chair and was found there in the middle of the road just below Dawson's mill. He was helped to the infirmary on Harrison Road, where it was thought his bladder was shot through. Two men from Ovenden, known to be injured with rifle shot, would not go for aid. There will have been many more.

'Many a tale of wounded men lying out in barns and under hedges was told', wrote Francis Grundy, 'but the Plug Rioting was at an end'.[200] The events of August 1842 were demonstrations with revolutionary possibilities in which thousands upon thousands of workers participated. At Halifax there were some who certainly had well formed objectives in mind. Papers recovered by police constable James Feather were, he said, taken from a committee calling itself the Property Committee, presumably formed to deal with the distribution of property after the people's takeover.[201]

Not just at Halifax, but over these same days Huddersfield was visited by marchers from Saddleworth, Oldham and Ashton who, after being described as 'calm, but resolute and determined' were, along with local demonstrators, dealt with in the streets by the Lancers, 'cutting indiscriminately … all in their way'.[202] At Bradford, crowds were dispersed at Lister's mill on Manningham and later at the mills by the canal side; then news reached the magistrates that fifty thousand were approaching from Keithley, Bingley, Howarth and Wilsden. This crowd was met by the authorities at Manningham Lodge, they were scattered across the wheat fields and disarmed in peacemeal fashion as they walked on into the town.[203]

At Leeds, on Monday 15th, at about the time that the Lancashire marchers first appeared in Halifax, two thousand people met on Hunslet Moor and, in orderly fashion, passed a resolution in favour of the Charter, then, the next day, they stopped mills at Claverley, Stanningley, Bramley and Pudsey where the military chose not to engage a crowd which had swollen far beyond a mere two thousand.[204] No conflict occurred at Sheffield, the adopted town of George Julian Harney, and Wakefield remained peaceful despite alarm when 'a large number of operative Colliers' entered the town.[205]

And so the marching, the meetings and speeches, the planned disabling of mills, the blood-spilling and the awful suffering, all came to nothing. Perhaps because of its mill owners, who had resisted earlier attempts at factory reform, no Yorkshire town experienced quite so dramatically the feelings of its people as Halifax did on the 15th and 16th August 1842. And no Yorkshire town's people experienced in quite so intense a fashion the violence of military might.

On Wednesday 17th August, the day after the military's attack upon the turn outs at Haley Hill, the surviving Halifax magistrate, George Pollard, wrote a report, in near to indecipherable handwriting, to the Home Secretary James Graham. George Pollard briefly described the Salterhebble attack to the Home Secretary. His description of the events which took place on Haley Hill later that afternoon is sketchy also. 'About four in the afternoon', he wrote, 'placards having been posted in the streets and carried through them by men on long poles, warning strangers to go home directly and the inhabitants to shut up their houses, the Magistrates being determined at all hazards to clear the town, the infantry about 80 in number, and 22 Dragoons started [out] for that purpose and about 1000 to 1500 Ruffians armed with bludgeons having past a few minutes before and on moving forward we met with a good deal of resistance and shortly after, the Infantry were fired upon ... [F]ive solders were hit with slugs, but thank God, not materially hurt, the five were returned as quick[ly] as possible; but we have not heard that anyone was killed. Soon after this a volley of stones was thrown at the Infantry ... when the infantry again fired without any immediate death taking place — the force then returned to the Police office with 30 to 40 prisoners, and there paraded the streets, and finding everything peaceable and quiet, they returned about 7 o'clock to their Barracks.[206]

In George Pollard's account to the Home Secretary, five soldiers were hit with slugs in an attack at some indeterminate time and place after four o'clock that afternoon. The *Halifax Guardian* mentioned that, 'some of them were shot with slugs in the back'. The report becomes more specific when going on to say how, in the grounds of Jonathan Akroyd's house further up the hill from the Shade, 'The mob resisted for a time, and several blunderbusses were seen among them. Some of the soldiers were hit by the slugs fired at them, but owing to the unskilfullness of the men who had fired the pieces, none did any serious damage'. One Lieutenant Hoey was hit in the back by one of the slugs, 'but obtained little or no injury'.[207] There was also mention in the *Halifax Guardian* of, 'private Neagle, from whose back and head several slugs have been extracted'. The Northgate Hotel writer's report, received by the Leeds magistrates at six-thirty on the Tuesday evening, said one of the corporals accompanying the omnibuses to Elland that morning had been shot by a rioter from Elland Wood, but there is no corroboration and this is likely to be a confusion with another, more widely reported, fatal injury sustained by one of the crowd through military fire at Salterhebble.

Official reports list seven injured on the afternoon of August 16th, these being injuries to members of the public. Samuel Crowther the nailmaker shot on King Street, Samuel Bates a weaver, Jonathan Booth the stonemason, John Holroyd bayoneted on Broad Street, William Sutcliffe, John Brook, Henry Walton, and an unnamed man; all were officially reported injured, at least two fatally, by bullets, bayonet or sabre cuts.[208] Names to add to these are those mentioned in newspaper reports; Matham Crook from Boothtown, Sutton Briggs, shot while standing on the hillside overlooking the Shade, and Charles Taylor cut by a sabre. Three other, un-named men were later found dead in Jonathan Akroyd's grounds.[209] Many of the men who were arrested that day were also injured. Then there was the significant number of injured and eventually dead who were not named or reported at all. The exact number of fatalities and injuries from that day will never be known but a conservative estimate of no less than six men killed that afternoon can be made. Many of the townspeople viewed the 'conduct of the military as ferocious'.[210]

13

The Aftermath (1842)

Of the men arrested on Tuesday 16th August, one was John Hodgson, the Chartist weaver who had knocked in the plugs at Haigh's mill the day before, also John Sutcliffe one of Haigh's workers, and the weaver William Jackson Cockroft who had entered Akroyd's mill. In all, twenty-seven men working in the cloth trade were arrested of which number eight were released the next day. Also arrested from other trades were Robert Rideough, a grinder of Charlestown, and William Jagger, a cooper. Joseph Pearson and Samuel Farrar, both delvers, were arrested. Also taken were John Farrar blacksmith, John Murphy a discharged soldier, and two miners, George Pitchforth from Elland and William Cawthray of Ovenden. William Cawthray was released the next day.[211] All these men lived in Halifax parish and many of them were injured. The Halifax police-house was as much a hospital as a prison. Fourteen men were sent on to York gaol the next morning.

Miners are under-represented in the lists of arrested, but this did not mean they were inactive. After their unexpected meeting at Halifax on the first day of the month, they had been going about things in their own way and on Monday 15th August, while other workers were battling with the authorities in their respective towns, the Yorkshire miners met at the Music Saloon, in Wakefield, to discuss their future. Their mass entry into the city had alarmed residents. The meeting's chairman was a Halifax man, Samuel Mann, who said that 'a certain newspaper', meaning the *Halifax Guardian*, had hinted, 'that their object was not so much to obtain an advance of wages as to stop machinery'.[212] Samuel Mann reiterated their purpose, which was to advance wages. A resolution was passed that only political resolutions which advocated the interests of the mining trade should be allowed, which alluded to the Chartists, whereupon John Wilkinson, who had come from Catherine Slack, a mile or two up from Boothtown, proposed that the delegates should be allowed to speak freely on social and political points. After these preliminaries, it was moved that the coal miners should form a national society.

This was the beginning the Miners' Association of Great Britain and Ireland; a significant moment in working people's history. But the heat of the day in this intensely hot summer of 1842 disturbed this seminal moment. Everyone decided to move outside where a large crowd was 'clamouring to gain admittance', and where it was cooler. The meeting continued out in the open space between the Music Saloon and the Court House where Samuel Mann, with the speakers, stood atop a wall to address the miners. There were close to two thousand there.

Jonas Jowett, a Bradford man, said that in the city, 'coal was selling at 3s 6d a ton and people were not content with it at that price, but wanted it cheaper than colliers could afford to get it'. He called for 'a union of men and masters'. 'If we and the masters do not unite, we cannot get our wages risen. We have the key in our own hands. Let us only cease to work and what will then become of the nation?'[213] His speech was received with cheers. Someone suggested their next meeting should be at Bradford, but it was resolved to keep to Wakefield.

There were Chartists there who mounted the wall once Samuel Mann had vacated it. They proposed that everyone present 'should not work any more until the Charter became the law of the land', but, typically for a meeting of miners, the crowd was already dispersing. And so, on Monday 15th August, while Halifax and Huddersfield were in the grip of violence, and while mills were stopped at Bradford, Leeds, Skipton, Keithley and Dewsbury, and while at Barnsley great crowds cheered for the Charter, at Wakefield no conflict occurred as the Yorkshire miners considered what they should do.

Thirty-six hours after this, William Sutcliffe's leg was amputated at Halifax Infirmary, and Jonathan Booth, after being visited by the vicar of Halifax Parish Church, died from his rifle shot injuries a little before ten o'clock on the evening of Wednesday 17th August.

At the Fleet prison in London, Richard Oastler very soon heard of the riots in Yorkshire. He often received visitors, many of whom were raising a fund to pay-off the £2,000 debt to Thomas Thornhill, including the accumulating interest. What must he have thought and felt at hearing of the terrible events in his home county while he was kept away? 'Have the tumultuary movements in the North taken me by surprise?', he wrote in his open letter, 'No, indeed they have not. They are the natural results, as I have forewarned you, of ... that passion for accumulation, which has no limits – of the fundamental principles of the Free Trade Theory, that "to give capital a fair remuneration, the price of labour *must* be kept down".[214] He urged the workers to solve their difficulties through a return to the old ways:

> CEASE FROM THE UNEQUAL STRIFE! By resisting the Queen's troops you will cause greater calamity to yourselves! There is a God – pour out your complaints to him ... Go to the relieving officers, and ... demand parish relief like men! Be civil, be courteous, but be *firm*. If they refuse, [go] to the magistrates. If those turn a deaf ear to your demands, then go to the Lords Lieutenant ... They will be sure to interfere, and see that your legal RIGHT is granted, or they will shake the security of their own property, and prove traitors to their Queen! ... Well, it is possible after all, that relief may be refused, *except in the workhouses*. Never mind that ... YES, FILL THE BASTILES TO OVERFLOWING ... When all the Bastiles are crowded, depend on it the Poor Law Commissioners will soon be discharged.[215]

After the great disturbances in Yorkshire of 15th and 16th August 1842, life returned to the way it had been before. In fact by Thursday 18th August, many mills in Yorkshire's industrial towns had started work again and by the following Monday just about all the mills were back to normal working in Halifax and its surrounding townships. But the authorities cautiously swore-in more special constables over the intervening weekend.

> [N]early 300 special constables have been sworn-in today for the townships of Greetland and Ovenden; which includes 37 of the mill-hands of Messrs. Balmforth's mill, Marshall-hall, who are sworn-in for the protection of the building and machinery by which they earn their daily bread. By thus protecting the honest labourer the designing demagogues are robbed of their dupes ...[216]

A reasonable proportion of special constables was, indeed, drawn from the working population. In Huddersfield, the owners of Starkie's and Armitage's mills had their men walk 'in a body' to the George Inn to take the special's oath.[217] Many of Jonathan Akroyd's Halifax workers also took the oath so that they could legally defend his mill and house. And from Shelf, a good number of working men volunteered their services because, the *Halifax Guardian* says, they were fed-up with people from Lancashire coming to tell them what to do.

The Halifax magistrates posted a second placard on Friday the 19th which read:

> [T]he magistrates earnestly exhort those mill owners who have not already set their mills to work, to do so immediately, and to furnish their workmen with arms, and also to instruct them ... should anyone attempt to touch the plugs of their boilers ... to give such person, or persons notice, that if they do not instantly desist, the consequences will be fatal, as they have received orders from their masters ... to protect their property at all hazards ... [T]his will, of course, have a stronger moral influence over the minds of those deluded creatures calling themselves "Chartists" than even the military protection which the magistrates have at their command ...[218]

This nicely shows the multifarious loyalties, pressures, motivations and manipulations which were in play during this time. Workers could choose to join the strikers or stick with their employers and keep their jobs and bread on the table for themselves and their children. Which way you went would depend on which fire burned in your belly; anger or prudence. The choice must be made, one way or the other. This division between families, which the authorities did not fail to use to their advantage, would produce bad feeling between neighbours. In war, the tactic of divide your enemy is an effective one. The turn-outs who were shot at and then restrained by special constables on Tuesday 16th in Jonathan Akroyd's grounds were said to have sworn blood for blood.[219] A comment made by Thomas Vevers' applies to special constables and regular soldiers alike: 'it was the labouring class', he said, 'that made the tyrants so strong, by being such fools as to enlist and fight their battles'.[220]

And so the Halifax strike, having reached a climax, from now on quite quickly faded away. 'The struggle', said Benjamin Wilson, 'was short but fierce'.[221] Not so in Lancashire. The Manchester weavers stayed out until late September. They kept away from their workplaces for seven weeks during which time each man received at most four pennies a week from a strike fund. Even if the industrial machinery had been stopped, the established social machinery was too great for the hundreds of thousands of protesters to overcome it. By October, the Attorney General, Frederick Pollock, who said the leaders of the strike had formed 'the most formidable conspiracy that ever existed', had instituted trials to punish whomever he could.[222]

There had been one positive national response to the terrible sufferings of the textile workers in the form of the Manufacturer's Relief Committee, brought together earlier in the year by royal appointment in that telling month of May 1842. Of all the districts in the country to receive relief, the '4425 destitute persons at Ovenden' received the lowest contributions in the land from this fund, that is, four pence and one farthing, due, the writer thought, to the 'imperfect judgment of the individual Members who might be present'.[223] There is no telling how things stood with Benjamin Rushton and his ailing wife.

Something else which made itself felt at this time was the Coal Mines and Collieries Regulation Act, powered by the evidence gathered by Samuel Scriven and his associates and which had just become law. Now, boys under the age of ten and all girls and women were no longer allowed to work down coal mines. If those politicians opposed to the Act had not managed to secure amendments favourable to themselves, the Bill also would have ensured that Patience Kershaw's two young brothers, Bethel and Solomon, would no longer have been allowed to work as hurries. But those amendments ensured that Bethel and Solomon continued to work in the mines. Not so Patience. The Act would save her from that terrible toil but also would lose her a valuable income. Patience's wage as a hurrier at 8s 6d a week represented about one sixth of her family's weekly wage and, compared to the cloth workers around her, was a very good wage. There would be some lead time before Patience would have to give up her life down Boothtown Colliery and, judging by her comments to Samuel Scriven, she would not be sorry for it. But she would have to find other employment with which she would not be familiar and to which, at first, she would not be suited.

Patience's near neighbour and contemporary from across the valley, John Snowden, was brought back to Halifax on the afternoon of Saturday 27th August, eleven days after being taken to Wakefield gaol upon his arrest. He was finally released at Halifax on 'entering in recognizance of £20 and one surety of £10 ... to keep the peace for twelve months', for which payment a fund must have been raised. In later years John Snowden would enjoy recalling how the Wakefield prison chaplain asked each prisoner to read from the Bible so that he could judge their level of education and, at his turn, he chose James 5:1, 'Go to now, ye rich men, weep and howl for your miseries that shall come upon you', which he hoped would discomfit the chaplain. By this time Benjamin Rushton, who was lecturing as far afield as Keithley on behalf of, 'persons suffering confinement', and Christopher Shackleton, also had been taken into custody by the Halifax authorities after the disturbances and a number of those men who had stopped the miners at Boothtown Colliery had been arrested. James Bawden was one, also Helliwell Shackleton, George Hemsley and John Isles. The town's prisons, reported the *Halifax Guardian*, 'are therefore again filled and sittings of the magistrates prolonged'.[224]

Halifax's magistrates' office, on Wards End, really was too small to comfortably accommodate so much activity, but at least, in the week following Halifax's riots and demonstrations, John Rhodes Ralph and John Rawson returned from London and were able to take much of the work from the shoulders of their colleagues. 'We continue to hear of the applications of wounded men to surgeons in the country', said the *Guardian*, 'and it would be very desirable if the magistrates could procure returns of each case'.

Shortly after the August riots, rumours began to circulate that a

plan to raise a local military force was being encouraged by Lord
Harewood, the county's Lord Lieutenant. This was received with such
enthusiasm by the Halifax and Huddersfield middle-classes that a local
regiment known as the Morley and Agbrigg Yeomanry Cavalry was
formed which, a few months later, became the 2nd West York Regiment
of Yeomanry Cavalry. They wore blue and seem to have been the only
Yeomanry corps in the country armed with carbines.[225]

Legacy

14

The Miners Unite (1842)

Patience Kershaw's testimony, printed alongside other details of the Mining Commissioners' reports in the *Halifax Guardian* during May 1842 must, surely, have provided the publicity necessary to encourage the miners of Halifax to come together early in August 1842. The published Commission had produced such an immense stirring of feeling throughout the whole town that it would have acted as a catalyst to the people on which it focused.

As a whole, the miners of northern England found they shared two major grievances. One was the truck system. This was the owners' system of payment by which they paid their miners in goods at their own stores instead of cash. The second was the bond system. The bond system tied miners to an employer for twelve months without the assurance of steady work or wages and which, legally, favoured the employer who, if in breach, was guilty only of a civil offence while for the miner it was a criminal one.[226] Miners were likely to find themselves imprisoned if they broke their working agreement. And now the mine owners were attempting to reduce payment through the enlargement of the corves while paying the same rate per load. This caused great anger. How greatly the work of the children, the hurriers, would be affected by the introduction of larger and heavier corves seems not to have been considered by miner or owner.

The Wakefield meeting of August 15th produced a published address from the Yorkshire coalminers to all consumers. 'Ladies and Gentlemen', it began:

> We, the colliers of Yorkshire ... are driven ... to lay before the public our grievances.
> 1st A reduction of wages to an alarming extent, so that we and our families are perishing for lack of food.
> 2nd A great addition has been made to our day's work, but none to our wages; (the reverse) we have as much coal to get in two days as we had formerly in three.
> 3rd On account of the corves (or waggons) being continually enlarged,

and our day's work increased, we have only two or three days in the week; the wages of two or three days is not sufficient to maintain us and our families through seven days.

4th We are obliged to work in water and damp places, so that we get rheumatism and all sorts of complaints; and we are obliged to work naked, or nearly so, on account of the hard and laborious employment we have to perform.

5th Getting coals by measure and selling them by weight; this is the reason that they are continually enlarging the corves; every new one that is made is larger than the old one. When they sold by measure they did not do so; if they had, the public would have got the benefit; but now that they pocket it all they are never quiet.

6th Our masters have turned off from their employment some of the delegates whom we chose to represent our grievances to them.

Look at our children; who takes care of them? … They are brought up in slavery and ignorance … They are doomed to follow their fathers in the pits, and crawl where he cannot … Are Englishmen to suffer slavery at home while they give millions of pounds and millions of Bibles to extirpate it from Asia, Africa and America; and send teachers to form schools in all parts of the globe, whilst our own children are remaining in ignorance, and grovelling in the bowls of the earth, under one of the most tyrannical and oppressive systems that ever existed?[227]

The Miners' Association of Great Britain and Ireland was founded six weeks after the publication of this address, on 7th November 1842, at Wakefield, less than three months after the great strike action. 'Its size, structure and intention made it, in many ways, the prototype of the modern trade union … [it] was an object of awe in its day'.[228] David Swallow was its general secretary and in these early days he applied to Feargus O'Connor for encouragement and legal advice which he received. It was the first union ever to go to law to protect its members, for which purpose it retained the services of a lawyer, W. P. Roberts, who also was a Chartist.[229] Once it became clear to them that they were up against laws designed to favour the employer, the association turned to political activism. In 1844, the Miners' Association raised its own petition of two million signatures in opposition to the greater empowerment of magistrates to imprison workers in cases of industrial dispute. By this time the union had a membership exceeding 60,000.

But they, and all the trades, were up against something as insubstantial yet as powerful as religious belief. They were up against an idea called Political Economy and its premise is made perfectly clear in the views of the intelligentsia and ruling classes who thought, 'the chief laws of Political Economy, however darkly they may lead to their result, are as unchangeable as those of nature, and it would be as possible to make the quicksilver in the thermometer expand beyond the temperature of its atmosphere as to fix wages at any other rate than that at which [they] would fix themselves',[230] and the chief laws of 'Political Economy' were that a decreasing population and increasing profits were the only levers to an improved life for workers. Not a good scenario for the workers. Put another way, too many workers meant not enough work for everyone so, logically, a little bit of natural wastage was an inevitable result; too little profit to the employers meant reduction in work availability and wages so, logically, protection of the capitalists' interest was the paramount object. It is this philosophy which led to the hated New Poor Law of 1834, to opposition to the Ten Hours Bill, the Mines and Collieries Bill, and to all other attempts to humanise industry. Unchallenged, it pandered to economic greed and self-interest. It is a philosophy which made itself felt amongst the majority of people without their knowing of its existence under the grand name of Political Economy.

The inmates of workhouses throughout the country would feel the effects of Political Economy well enough. Having reached the extremity of survival, they worked at whatever task was given them for whatever dietary remuneration the workhouse masters deemed fit. The London Commissioners set the ethos, and it was severe. At Halifax the workhouse paupers were kept alive on a weekly diet of porridge, four pints of soup, nineteen ounces of bread, potatoes, cooked meat twice and lobscouse, which comprised stewed meat, vegetables and ships biscuits. The Halifax Guardians replaced the lobscouse with suet pudding in the first month of

1843, which was an improvement contrary to the Commissioners' rules.[231]

Mary Rushton, Benjamin Rushton's wife, who had severe physical hardships of her own to endure during these months, succumbed to her illness on Monday, 8th May 1843, when she died at their cottage at Friendly Fold. She was fifty-seven. 'She was a true patriot, a good neighbour, a tender mother, and a faithful and dutiful wife', wrote the *Northern Star*.[232] Mary Rushton, née Helliwell, was buried on 11th May 1843, at St. Mary's Church in Illingworth. She did not leave her husband entirely alone. Their son Zimri appears to have lived with him at Friendly Fold at least until 1851, and he had other children and grandchildren in the cottage or living close by.

In the autumn months of 1842 the Chartist movement had fallen into a difficult position. The strike action had left it no nearer to achieving a universal franchise and its path forward was more and more obscured. Hundreds of its supporters had been put into prison, some had been sentenced to deportation, and now the turn had come of fifty-nine of its leading personalities, including Feargus O'Connor and George Julian Harney, to face the law. These men were obliged to travel to Lancaster at the beginning of March the following year to attend their trial on nine charges of seditious conspiracy intending to 'bring about a change in the laws and constitution of this realm, against the peace of our said Lady the Queen, Her Crown and Dignity'. Their trial ran for eight days and the judge, Robert Monsey Rolfe, who suffered from a flu-like ailment during the entire week, gave his summing up on 9th March, after which the jury brought verdicts of not guilty on twenty-one of the defendants, and guilty on various single counts for the remainder. Feargus O'Connor was found guilty of having endeavoured 'to excite Her Majesty's liege subjects to disaffection and to persuade and encourage [them] to unite, confederate, and agree to leave their ... employments'.[233] The fear of a second spell of imprisonment for him, just two years after being released from York, was dispelled on a technical point later in the year.

And so ends the story of the strike of 1842. It was a water-shed event in the lives of a great many. For the majority it must have represented an effort of mountainous proportions to change the established way of things. The August meeting of the trades at Manchester had resolved that no-one should return to work until the Charter was won. This was an aim they had thought achievable and their disillusionment, when the strike faded away without measurable result, must have been terrible. For the Chartist leadership it represented an absolute failure for they had associated themselves utterly with the workers' strike; they had encouraged it and harnessed it to their cause for universal voting rights. Whatever they might have hoped to gain, the Chartist leadership really did stick its neck out over the strikes.

Was it all to no purpose? Absolutely not. The events of 1842, at Halifax and elsewhere, can justly be viewed as an uprising of the oppressed. In Britain it would take time not violence to bring change. But attempted revolts are indispensible to the thought which shapes times to come.

15

The Passage of the Ten Hours Bill (1830-1847)

The times which were to come were very slow in coming. The fight against factory slavery went on for many more years. By 1830, modest legislation had applied for some years to cotton mills, but there was 'nothing to control the running of the other major textile industry', the woollen and worsted manufactories. 'Why should not children working in them be protected by legislative enactments as well as those who work in cotton mills?' Richard Oastler had asked. Until he was told of it in 1830 by his friend, John Wood, a Bradford mill owner, he had no idea of how bad working conditions were in the mills at Bradford, Halifax and Huddersfield. The knowledge of it so horrified him that he immediately wrote a letter headed, 'Slavery in Yorkshire' which, after some difficulty, was eventually printed in the *Leeds Mercury* on 16th October 1830.

> Thousands of our fellow creatures and fellow subjects , both male and female, the miserable inhabitants of a *Yorkshire Town*; ... are this very moment existing in a state of slavery *more horrid* than are the victims of that hellish system – *"Colonial Slavery."* ... The very streets which receive the dropping of an "Anti-Slavery Society" are every morning wet by the tears of the innocent victims at the accursed shrine of avarice, who are *compelled* (not by the cart whip of the negro slave driver) but by dread of the equally appalling thong or strap of the overlooker, to hasten ... to those magazines of Infantile Slavery *the Worsted Mills in the Town and Neighbourhood of Bradford!!* Would that I had [the] eloquence, that I might rouse the hearts of the nation, and make every Briton swear "These innocents shall be free!"[234]

Richard Oastler finished his letter with this: 'The nation now is most resolutely determined that [enslaved] Negroes shall be free. Let them however, not forget that Britons have common rights with Africa's sons'. John Cam Hobhouse, MP for Westminster, submitted a Bill to Parliament proposing reduced working hours and an extension of the legislation to woollen and worsted mills. It was an attempt to bring rational controls to the rampant phase of an industrial community unused to any kind of restriction. The mining industry, underground and out of sight, remained entirely out of mind until Lord Ashley's revelatory commission of 1841.

All this while, Jonathan Akroyd was making his fortune from the unregulated processing of worsteds. He opposed John Cam Hobhouse's Bill which proposed extended legislation to his operations. Jonathan Akroyd was a Liberal in political terms, a chapel-goer and a supporter of education for his working people, but he could not bring himself to accept any state imposed legislation to his business practices. The idea appalled him. His grandfathers had miraculously risen from the normal ranks of Halifax hillside weavers and combers and he believed, absolutely, in unfettered commercial enterprise. He vehemently opposed restrictive legislation and remained perfectly comfortable in the knowledge that his massive fortune rested upon the labour of more than a thousand of Halifax's unprotected children.

And so it is no surprise to find Halifax's mill owners, of whom Jonathan Akroyd and his brother James carried particular influence, obstructing Oastler's factory improvement campaign in 1831. When, by this campaign, child labour became a strong political issue, Bradford's and Manchester's owners were at least open to the idea of some restrictive legislation. It was the Halifax and Glasgow industrialists who stood out as main opposers to any external interference. At a meeting on 5th March 1831, held at the Old Cock Inn and chaired by James Akroyd, Halifax's textile mill owners resolved that 'this Meeting views with alarm':

> The measures proposed in the House of Commons, to Curtail the Hours
> of Labor [sic] in Mills and Factories, and to limit the Age of Children
> employed in the same.[235]

Their reasons, which they set out in fourteen points, include the claim that to work in their mills is not 'injurious to the Health and Comforts of this class of Operatives, and that the present term of Labor (vis. 12 Hours per Day) is not attended with any consequences injurious to those employed'. Also, according to these men, controlled restriction of working hours would raise prices to their consumers and damage the prosperity of the district by reducing their trade competitiveness; the effects of such legislation would harm the lives of the operatives through a consequent reduction in wages. The meeting claimed that 'the Character of the generality of Master Worsted Spinners in respect to Humanity, Kindness, and considerate Attention to those in their employ is unimpeachable' and asserts that it is 'convinced of the pernicious tendency and effects of all *Legislative Enactments*, whether Protective or Restrictive, which propose to regulate the details of Trade and Manufacture'.

The fact is that the life expectancy of working people in Halifax was less than half that of their employers. Twenty-two years of age was soon to become the average at death for Halifax's mill workers.[236] One of Jonathan Akroyd's contemporaries mentions 'the very severe nature' of injuries in the town, 'arising from the complicated state of machinery'. In the first four decades of the 1800s a good number of the 80,346 cases taken to the Halifax Dispensary for treatment in those years would be industrial injuries.[237]

Besides the Akroyds, the Dawson, Holdsworth and Crossley families were represented at the Old Cock Inn meeting that day and, with the extraordinary power they had at their command, they succeeded, in following months, in seeing off any extension of government legislation to all woollen and worsted manufactories. As one Halifax historian puts it, the Akroyds were 'the most bitter opponents of legislation', in whose mills, 'the worst conditions, the most cowed operatives' existed.[238] Lord Ashley's phrase 'ready and happy self-delusion' might best describe their position. Richard Oastler said of industrialists like Jonathan Akroyd that, 'he would rather be under the control of a she-wolf than under such Christians'.[239] These circumstances illuminate the strikers' concentration on Akroyd's mill at Haley Hill during August 1842, and the especially strong local feeling which exploded into violence against the authorities at Salterhebble.

A Ten Hours Act was eventually passed, but not until 1847; in 1831, Richard Oastler still had another sixteen years to go. At the start, he persuaded Michael Sadler to take up the fight in parliament, and then Lord

Ashley. Ashley presented a Ten Hours Bill in 1833 which actually included the condition that an employer was to be imprisoned if he violated its terms more than three times. This was too much, even for those manufacturers who supported him, and Ashley withdrew the condition. In fact his whole Bill was far too much for far too many and, during 1833, political manoeuvrings within parliament scuppered its chances. These political manoeuvrings were led by Lord Althorp who undermined Ashley's Bill simply by asking for another investigation into conditions in the factories, after which a fresh Bill would replace Ashley's original. Lord Althorp was, however, obliged to introduce a Bill under this agreement which he did in the same year. His Factory Bill of 1833 provided for a working day of nine hours for children under thirteen in textile mills, and twelve hours a day for those between thirteen and eighteen years. It never worked. The manufacturers got around its conditions very easily, as the Halifax surgeon, James Holroyd, soon discovered.

And so the fight went on.

"When the House in its wisdom and mercy decided that 45 hours in a week was a term of labour long enough for an adult negro [slave], I thought it would not have been unbecoming ... if we had considered *whether 69 hours a week were not too many for the children of the British Empire*", said Lord Ashley to parliament on 20th July 1838.[240] Here he is, five years on from his defeated original Ten Hours Bill, still trying to have the ten hours principle considered, at the very time that the Chartist movement first galvanised British workers. It would take nine years after this before a ten hour working day for women and children was brought to bear on textile manufacturers. It was passed in 1847 and made effective on 1st May 1848. Immense personal and political labour from dedicated men had continued from 1830 to 1847 simply to reduce the working hours of children and their mothers to ten a day in the textile industries. Strangely, the equally significant Mines and Collieries Regulation Act had emerged, almost as an aside, to this effort. The enterprise had been gargantuan and the price of such tenacity not small.

Richard Oastler certainly paid the price. Eighteen months after the great strike of 1842 he was released from four years of imprisonment. In February 1844, he made his way up to Yorkshire and on the night of Monday 19th, he slept at the Railway Hotel at Brighouse. Upon waking the next morning the night's frost had cleared, the day dawned sharp and bright. By late morning workers and their children, some carrying union jacks and others small white flags, had arrived outside the hotel. Everyone inside could see that his years in prison had affected him very much. He looked 'pale and care-worn'. They held a reception and made speeches in the hotel's main room. Lawrence Pitkeithly celebrated with the rest who had come to mark the occasion. Also there was Bradford's George Stringer Bull, who had recruited Lord Ashley to the Ten Hours campaign on Richard Oastler's behalf eleven years earlier.

By early afternoon thousands of people were gathered outside the Railway Hotel, along with 'several excellent bands of music'. Everyone began to make their way to Huddersfield and from Netheroyd Hill the 'immense procession was seen to the best advantage':

> As the solid, living mass of human beings moved down the hill – the tossing white banners – the peeling cheers of the multitude – the infantile shout of 'welcome' – the sweet strain of the music, now swelling in full chords, then dying away in distant melody – all these, combined with the absorbing thought that Richard Oastler was that day making his triumphal way into his own loved Huddersfield, made up a scene at once affecting and spirit-stirring.[241]

They came into the town by Northgate, passing along Cross Church Street, Queen Street, Ramsden Street and New Street, into Market Place and along Westgate and Temple Street. Richard Oastler then spoke to the crowd which congregated on the open ground before the Druid's Arms on the Halifax Road.

When his wife, Mary, whom he seems greatly to have loved, died little more than a year later, he left Yorkshire to live at Guildford in Surrey for a while. The love felt for him in Huddersfield did not fade and eventually funds were again raised to enable him to live in reasonable comfort at Harrogate, and there he, 'the King of the factory children', died in 1861.[242]

His purpose had been achieved, he had seen the passing of the Ten Hours Act. Karl Marx judged it to be, 'the first time that ... the political economy of the middle class succumbed to the political economy of the working class'.[243] But another aspect of 'Yorkshire Slavery', safety in working, was something to be fought for at another time.

The 1834 New Poor Law, which Richard Oastler had battled so passionately against, remained in place for almost one hundred years. Relief given to children, the sick and mentally disturbed was effectively taken from its purview in the interim years and its system slowly changed over that time. The withdrawal of outdoor relief was never universally applied. Finally, when the process of closing the workhouses was begun in 1929, children under the care of the authorities at Halifax were housed at Craigie Lea, in Ovenden.[244] Halifax's Workhouse was demolished in April 1972.[245]

16
The Ongoing Fight for the Vote

After 1842, the fight for the vote which everyone believed would provide the wherewithal to do away with Factory Slavery and other social injustices, went on for another eighty-six years. The Chartists survived, as a force to be reckoned with, for another six years after the affrays at Halifax. What mental pictures rise when thinking of Feargus O'Connor? In 1842 he was a man in his late-forties, and, for those times, a very tall man at nearly six feet. He was 'athletic', 'short-necked, 'iron framed'. He cut the figure of a gentleman. 'No member of the prize ring could fight his way with more desperate energy through a crowd than could this electioneering pugilist'. He had a broad, massive forehead 'though considerably deficient in the faculties of reflection', says one who knew him. He was 'eccentric'.[246] With his great talent for oratory and a voice which 'made the vault of Heaven echo with its sound', possibly due to his extremely short neck, he was able to carry masses of people with him, which he did; but after the events of 1842, he had to rethink his plans for the working people, their rights, and where he might lead them.

A land scheme seemed a good way forward to O'Connor, and he set to, to establish one, a little along the lines of the Owenite communities, or colonies, which were derided by just about everyone as pie-in-the-sky. Robert Owen had built a grandiose Hertfordshire mansion for his colonists to live in. Feargus O'Connor's scheme brought the possibility, through a ballot, of a cottage and plot of land to farm, and in Halifax there were some fifty subscribing members by 1848, one of whom was Benjamin Rushton.[247] But the Chartist Cooperative Land Society would not last long. It was something to keep the cause going while the fight for the vote languished.

The parliamentary vote which Feargus O'Connor had fought for was, of course, eventually won. It came in stages, over decades. Its genesis was the Chartist movement and its final achievement came long after Feargus O'Connor had left this world. 1848 was a remarkable year. It is the year of revolutions in France and in the Italian and German states, in Switzerland, Denmark, Hungary, Poland and the Ukraine. Also in Ireland some attempt was made, while a million died of starvation and those who did not, emigrated to America. It was a natural year for a third Chartist petition in Britain and O'Connor campaigned again with the help of twenty-nine-year-old Ernest Jones, a man new to the cause. Signatures were once again secured and the 1848 petition was collected in London, as others had been. People came from all across the country to be there and on Monday, 10th April great crowds paraded through London's streets towards Kennington Common where they rallied. They planned to make a united march on Westminster and the Houses of Parliament after the speeches were made. None there could have known with clarity that this was to be Chartism's last, great effort.

Photographer William Kilburn took his equipment to the common, set it up and took an image of the crowd. It is breathtaking. Flags fly on the hustings, everyone looks relaxed. There seem to be as many top hats as cloth caps. The top hats belonged to policemen. The photograph's sky over distant buildings has been coloured blue and, as that morning was a fine sunny one, was blue in reality. Before speeches, Police Commissioner Richard Mayne asked Feargus O'Connor to talk with him over by the Horns Tavern. Whatever was said between these two Irishmen, it dawned on the organisers that a mistake had been made in bringing the petition and crowds across to the south-side of the river because the authorities had secured the bridges northward, back to Westminster. Blackfriars Bridge as well as Waterloo, Hungerford and Westminster bridges were not passable. No procession could now accompany the Charter from the common to the Houses of Parliament.[248] While George Julian Harney and others addressed smaller groups gathered around the common, Feargus O'Connor and then Ernest Jones, the latter reluctantly, urged the bulk of the crowd to disperse peaceably, which it did.

Feargus O'Connor presented the Charter to parliament that evening but the presentation was odd; the Charter is reported to have contained a number of ridiculous signatures; 'Pugnose', 'Mr Punch', 'Queen Victoria'.

The entire document was ridiculed. This was the end of the Chartist hope. It was a great demoralisation. Some time later the 1848 Charter was officially dismissed by parliament.

Within four years Feargus O'Connor was showing signs of mental illness. This ailment had been affecting him for some time, perhaps to some degree as early as 1848. As his mental health deteriorated, the Chiswick House Asylum run by Thomas Harrington Tuke became his home for some time until he removed to his sister Harriet's house at Notting Hill. Less than two weeks after this he died, on 30th August 1855. He was sixty-one years old. At his death the vote for working people was no nearer than it had been twenty years before, despite his mighty efforts during those years.

And still the fight for the vote went on. Ernest Jones, who stood with Feargus O'Connor on the hustings at Kennington, came onto the scene four years after the 1842 strike and was highly regarded as a Chartist leader. He was a lawyer dedicated to the people's cause, a poet, a novelist and a man who linked the old order with the new, one of the threads which runs from the struggling Chartist movement of 1848 to the Reform Act of 1867 when the process of real change would, at last, begin. Ernest Jones had come, quite suddenly, to Chartism, almost as if it were a religious awakening. He says of his own Chartist poems 'I am pouring the tide of my songs over England ... I thank God I am prepared to rush fresh and strong into the strife or struggle of a nation'.[249]

Halifax was his home-from-home, his centre of operation. He was as strongly associated with Halifax as Richard Oastler was with Huddersfield. Ernest Jones stood as a Chartist parliamentary candidate for Halifax at the general election of 1847. This made a great change from the usual Tory and Whig contests. A workers' representative was standing and this was a new thing. 'Meetings were held nightly', Benjamin Wilson said, 'excitement was great'.

> There was a tea party in connection with it for which the women had made preparations, and they were determined that the radical colour should be well represented on the occasion. I was at the first sitting down

which was largely composed of women. Some had their caps beautifully decorated with green ribbons, others had green handkerchiefs, and some even had green dresses.[250]

The vast majority in Halifax preferred Ernest Jones over the Tory and Whig candidates, but of course, those with a vote to cast preferred the Tory and Whig over Ernest Jones. Out of the four candidates, he received twelve percent of the votes having taken Halifax by storm when, earlier in the month, he 'addressed the electors and non-electors at one of the most crowded meetings ever held in the Odd Fellows Hall, and wor[e] away the prejudices of all parties; so that Whigs, Tories and Radicals, have alike given in their names as supporters to the cause'.[251] People gathered in the streets and courts, even on the rooftops of Halifax to hear him speak. But it was the Tory and Whig candidates who gained seats in parliament that year, not the people's choice, Ernest Jones.

It was during these election campaigns that Jonathan Akroyd died, suddenly and publicly, at the Northgate Hotel. As a supporter of education for the masses he had agreed to chair a meeting on the morning of Monday 26th July on that subject, in support of the Liberal candidate Charles Wood, at the Northgate where a great crowd of workmen and their sons, now hostile to the Liberal message, was gathering. Some of the crowd went round to the back of the building, entered through a rear door and came noisily across the platform towards those making their way in from the front. Things were already out of hand. When Jonathan Akroyd and Charles Wood entered the room they were cheered by their supporters and, due to the greater support of Ernest Jones, were received by even more boos. This was a surprising turn of events for the Liberals. It was something they were not at all used to.

'My fellow townsmen', Jonathan Akroyd began, 'I sincerely hope that you will let us have order and peace'. The *Halifax Guardian* reporter records that he went on to ask the crowd:

> What has led you to rise up against our late faithful servants [the Liberal representative]? (hubbub and cat-calls). What is the ground, what is the cause, from whence this originates? (hisses, yells and great confusion).

136

Well, gentlemen, it has arisen out of what I call the most important and soundest measure ever proposed for the welfare of the labouring classes of this extensive town and parish ("No, no" "Yes, yes", and uproar). The foundation of this our position is exclusively and entirely upon the education measure. ("No" "Yes" and uproar) ... It is for the benefit of the labouring classes, for your children (uproar). It is for the removal of vice and ignorance from among us'.[252]

But there was no prevailing upon people who, quite simply, wanted a fair day's wage for a fair day's work. They did not want to be kept in their place with kindly offers of religion-based education. Notions of education to solve 'vice and ignorance' would be like a red rag to a bull. 'And, then' appealed Jonathan Akroyd, to these people who had turned alien, 'you dismiss your old and faithful servant'. The *Halifax Guardian* reporter observed that this was greeted with 'groans, strangely blended with yelling and whistling'. That 'old and faithful servant' was defunct. The working people now had their own representative and no longer felt that Jonathan Akroyd and his sponsored candidate Charles Wood, served their interests. Yet Jonathan Akroyd quite clearly felt that he and Charles Wood did. 'I lament -' uttered the beleaguered speaker but the rest of his words were, 'completely drowned amid the discordant noises of the room'.

One James Milligan then stood up in front of the crowd and pleaded for quiet and patience, after which Jonathan Akroyd resumed. 'I am, indeed, surprised that the working classes should have taken this matter up in the way they have (confusion) ...

Is it not necessary and important to enlighten the minds of the ignorant: and how all this opposition should arise to this most beneficial measure is to me one of the greatest anomalies I ever knew (uproar). It is to enlighten – (confusion, and cries of "order"). And why you have risen up against it in this way, is, to me most surprising.

He repeated these last words, "to me, most surprising", and these were the last words he ever would speak. Then, 'as if making a bow to the meeting, he fell forward upon the table'. Jonathan Akroyd died within a few minutes of his collapse. His astonishingly great fortune, which well exceeded a million pounds, and the running of the family business went to his son, Edward.

All this power-shifting-upset at Halifax, largely caused by the candidature of Ernest Jones, had taken place in the year before the Kennington Common rally, and it took no more than the passing of that year, after having worn away 'the prejudices of all parties' at Halifax during the 1847 election, for Ernest Jones to be arrested at Manchester, on 8th June 1848, on charges of sedition, unlawful assembly and riot for a speech given at Bonner's Fields in London. Remembering that 1848 was the year of European revolutions, during which the French disposed of Louis Philippe, it is no wonder the Chartists revived in this year and that the British government again took up an aggressively defensive position. The threat was so palpable that Queen Victoria quit the mainland for her house on the Isle of Wight as working men, Benjamin Rushton, Issac Clisset, John Snowden and Christopher Shackleton included, maintained that the British should aspire to 'a similar change' as the people of France.[253]

At Skircoat Green, Benjamin Wilson, now a young man of twenty-four, actually bought a gun and said it had become 'a common practice to march through the streets in military order ... Matters now began to look serious'.[254] Unemployment and destitution among the Halifax weavers and combers were extensive and dreadful at this time and the town's Relief Committee had at its disposal £100 a week, sufficient to provide a few pennies to each unemployed family to keep them from starvation.[255] There had been a Chartist meeting on Skircoat Moor on 21st April, just two weeks after the Kennington Common rally. People from Huddersfield, Northowram, Bradford and Leeds had come, many wearing tri-colour rosettes and carrying tri-colour flags, the Revolutionary French blue was substituted with British Radical green. One speaker said he was not afraid of physical force and, interestingly, thought that the middle classes were, 'prepared to assist the working class to a certain extent', but did not think they would come willingly.

At London, the Chartist Convention had decided to hold fast and form as an Assembly, as a nominal alternative government, until the workers' vote was won. Now, Isaac Clisset proposed that the Halifax Chartists …

> agreeing with the [Chartist] National Convention in its general conduct, and particularly in regards the election of a National Assembly, pledge itself to render that body all the support in its power'.[256]

This was another of those great moments. The optimistic expectation was that the Chartist Convention would lead the way, but it could not rise to the faith put in it. The government, on the other hand, did not hesitate to follow through with a final blow to its challengers. It was an easy matter for government machinery. It arrested Chartists and prosecuted many on poor evidence. Even when the prosecution's evidence did not stand up to scrutiny, many were still sentenced to long terms of imprisonment. 'Great God!' exclaimed *Northern Star* correspondent G.J. Clarke, who had just assisted Ernest Jones' wife to the railway station at Manchester after her husband's arrest by two London policemen, 'to what a state are we hastening when the right of public meeting is trampled upon [and] liberty of speech refused'.[257] Two years earlier, Benjamin Rushton in speaking of Ernest Jones, whom he was meeting for the first time, had foreseen how likely it was that, 'Government will strike him down with the strong arm of the law',[258] and now, Benjamin Rushton's fear justified, at Halifax, thousands 'congregated in the streets talking the matter over in groups, and it cast a gloom all over the town as Mr. Jones was very popular there'.[259]

1848 was the year in which the British government settled the matter of Chartism for good. Ernest Jones' experience in court and in prison cannot tell more clearly of the treatment endured by those who fought for social reform and were persecuted for it. At his London trial in July 1848, three months after the Kennington Common affair, he said people had learned that petitioning was no longer of any use and that 'they wished to demonstrate the public opinion by more apparent means'. He put it to the court: 'Follow out the links of your political chain in alternate cause and effect: Monopoly and Destitution, Discontent and Crime, Taxation and Insurrection … Behold, how you have grudged the poor their rights, which makes you fearful for your own! ... Instead of building workhouses, erect Colleges of Agriculture: instead of emigration, promote home colonisation ... You think Chartism is quelled. Learn that it is more strong than ever. While oppression reigns, Chartism resists. While misery lasts, Chartism shall flourish; and when misery ceases the Charter will be law'.[260]

After this speech he was sentenced to two years not just of imprisonment but of solitary confinement. G.D.H. Cole says the Chartist prisoners of 1848, 'were treated with barbarous severity — so much so that the two who were sentenced with Ernest Jones both died in prison'. The Halifax Chartists supported his wife and children during this time. Cole quotes a large portion of Ernest Jones' revelatory prison recollection, and here it is:

I was kept for more than two years in separate confinement on the silent system, most rigidly enforced - so rigidly that for an involuntary smile I was sent for three days to a dark cell on bread and water. For the first nineteen months I was kept without books, pen, ink, or paper, and had to sit out that time in a cell, twelve feet by seven, locked up in solitude and silence, without even a table or chair. To this cell (the day cell) were three windows, two without glass but with rough wooden shutters, through which the wind and snow and rain of winter blew all over the place. My night cell was of far smaller dimensions, 9 feet by 4 feet. Its window was unglazed – its shutters did not meet the window frame nor each other by one or two inches. There was an aperture over my bed 18 in. by 12 in., through which the snow and rain fell on me as I slept, saturating my clothes with moisture, so that often the water dripped from them as I put them on. The bed itself was a sack of straw with a piece of carpeting. From this bed I had to go, when I rose at five in the morning, across two yards in my shirt and trousers only, to wash and dress in the open air, after getting wet through in the rain and snow while dressing, and sitting all day in my wet clothes in my fireless cell; for during the first twelve months I was allowed no fire in my day cell. During the intense frost of the winter of '49, I had to break the ice in the stone trough in which I was compelled to wash, in the same water, frequently, that other prisoners had used. The diet was so poor, and often of so revolting a kind, that at last I was unable to walk across my cell without support, through lose of strength. Neither fork nor knife was allowed at meals, and I had to tear my food with my fingers. Bent to the ground with rheumatism, and racked by neuralgia, I applied for permission to have a fire, but this was denied me, as already stated, till the second year of my imprisonment. Then I became so weak that I was compelled to crawl on all fours if I sought to reach the door of my cell to knock for assistance. On one occasion I fell against the grate, and had a narrow escape of being burned to death. It will be remembered that in the year of 1849, the cholera raged so fearfully in London that in one day as many as 417 persons died. During the height of the plague, while suffering from bowel complaint, I was sent to a darkened cell, because I did not pick the oakum that was brought to me as my daily task ... During all this time, after the first few weeks, I was allowed to hear from my wife and children only once every three months... . Out of the four other political prisoners who were sentenced simultaneously with myself, two – Alexander Sharp and John Williams – died in prison after about six months' endurance of this treatment; and the coroners' juried in their verdicts attributed their early deaths to the sufferings they had undergone, censured the treatment, and recommended its discontinuance – but it was continued, unaltered, notwithstanding. The third, John Vernon, died soon after his release, which was granted him six months before the expiration of his sentence, after he had been eighteen months in prison ... I have recorded but a portion – a small portion – of the sufferings inflicted.[261]

Taking a few days, after his release, to recover sufficiently to travel to Halifax, Ernest Jones arrived by train at Sowerby Bridge on 15th July 1850. He was met by a great crowd of Chartists, along with three bands, seven cabs, and a carriage drawn by four greys, all led by a cart flying a red banner which read 'E.C. Jones Esq. The friend of the people' and on the other side 'Equality – Liberty – Fraternity'. George Julian Harney also was there to greet him, and the liberated man was driven in the carriage with Harney and his wife to West Hill Park, just up from the town centre where celebrations were planned, and through roads lined with thousands who had come out to see him pass. It was quickly realized that Ernest Jones was too frail to be able to cope with hours of ceremony, so an on-the-spot decision to split the single proceeding into two was made; one to be held early in the evening, the other mid-evening. He thanked everyone for their support of his wife Jane during his time in prison, 'while the rich, and titled, and aristocratic relatives of my wife and myself' he said, 'did nothing to alleviate her sufferings'.

> I have passed through the gates of my prison but I have not entered through the gate of liberty. I have passed from a prison where walls are narrow and the cells are small, into a large prison whose walls are water and whose keys are gold, and whose jailors are pride, prejudice, ignorance and superstition ... [a]nd in spite of their treatment of me the life is still pulsing and beating in my veins, and that life I dedicate to the people's cause.[262]

And so he did, even though the Chartists were diminished and demoralised by this time. At Halifax there was a determined group still working from a room at the back of Nicholl's Temperance Hotel on Broad Street. 'Our aim', wrote Benjamin Wilson much later, 'was to carry on the agitation by engaging such men as ... Gammage, and others to lecture in the town, but it appeared to be to no purpose for very few came to hear them'.[263]

'I feel convinced there are thirty years of health and life in me', Ernest Jones had told the crowd at West Hill Park in 1850. He had just two-thirds that number. He died in January 1869. But he did live long enough to see the passing of the Reform Act of 1867, which would double the numbers of electors in England and Wales. Benjamin Rushton, who was with him at West Hill Park on that summer's evening of 1850, would not.

17

An Alliance with the Middle Class

Ernest Jones remembers visiting Benjamin Rushton at his cottage at Friendly Fold, 'where still the loom was fixed, and there we saw this aged son of toil weaving the finest and most exquisite textures, at a time of life when he should have been resting in competence on the earnings of the past'.[264] Another, familiar with the life of the Bradford weavers over the hill, says that, 'many an older weaver had become as much attached to his favourite loom as a warrior to his old steed',[265] and this, perhaps, was true of Benjamin Rushton. By 1853 he had lived as a widower for ten years and on 17th June 1853, eleven years after the riots at Halifax, Benjamin Rushton followed his wife. He died in their cottage behind Friendly Fold.

For most of his life he had preached Methodist New Connexion principles and he was, throughout the various agitations which arose during his lifetime, as involved in religious life as he was in the political even though he grew increasingly anti-clerical during the 1830s and put political rights before chapel loyalty. Benjamin Rushton is the perfect example of a Chartist guided by his belief in the Christian message. 'He was highly respected by the Chartists of Yorkshire and Lancashire', says Benjamin Wilson, 'and was looked upon in this town and neighbourhood as... a leader amongst the Chartists since its commencement'.[266] Benjamin Rushton went about the business of lecturing, preaching, raising funds, chairing meetings and addressing vast crowds in a manner which affected his listeners in an uncommon way. His actions and the way in which they were recorded leave an impression of a man of great surety, fire and privacy. He may have left the world unaided by medical assistance, as his death certificate says he did, but his burial passed with immense attention.

The Halifax Chartist association ensured a public funeral for him. At mid-morning on the 26th of June 1853 they met on the field by the Northgate Hotel, where everyone had been invited to assemble by Ernest

Jones, before processing up to the cottage at Friendly Fold. There a contingent from Bradford joined those from Halifax. 'The sight was magnificent' recalls Benjamin Wilson. 'The coffin – a double one, covered with black cloth, and very elegant – was borne from the house at twelve o'clock' and carried by 'six veteran Chartists' to Lister Lane Cemetery. Tens of thousands came to Halifax for the funeral of Benjamin Rushton. His namesake says he saw, 'more people in Halifax that day than I had ever seen before or since, and the public funeral[s] that I have seen in this town have been a mere nothing in comparison to this'.[267] What does this say of the man who wrote nothing but spoke volumes at moments of historical importance?

Benjamin Rushton died before realistic hope even for an extended working-man's vote glimmered. The younger neighbour whom he left behind, John Snowden, says that 'for a time after 1848 the Chartist cause was at a great discount. Many who had previously shouted for it derided those who had been most conspicuous in it, to their shame be it said. Well, I did not despair'.[268] But he did despair. 'I am sorry to inform you that there is no Chartist organisation in Halifax nor in any of the numerous villages surrounding it' he wrote to Ernest Jones in 1859. The Chartists, he says, are so 'thoroughly disgusted at the indifference and utter inattention of the multitude to their best wishes that they too are resolved to make no more sacrifices in a public cause'.[269]

Nothing can express more profoundly the great disillusionment within local Chartist leadership or reveal more clearly the sense of resignation within the body of the people to the continuance of things as they were, following their monumental but unsuccessful attempts at change. After the efforts of the Welsh miners and iron workers to raise an insurrection in 1839, after the Midlands miners' and Northern factory workers' reaction to wage reductions which lead to the widespread strikes of all trades in 1842, after the briefly revived hopes of 1848, all these hopes of change, all were crushed by the time of the late 1850s. People seem to have given up.

But things changed. John Snowden, following a new trend adopted by his Chartist colleague Alexander Stradling who at this time said, 'I do not care how reform comes so long as it comes ...', joined forces with the formerly despised middle-class reformers and became involved in their movement for limited political reform.[270] And in this way, slowly, began the political change for which the Chartist stalwart Benjamin Rushton and his like-minded colleagues had fought. On Monday 11th March 1861 a Parliamentary Reform Association, dominated by middle-class men, met for the first time at Halifax in the Odd Fellows Hall, following on from Bradford's own a week or two before.[271] James Stansfeld, now Halifax's Liberal MP, sent a note to this meeting saying, 'We can do nothing whatever worth doing, here, on this question of reform unless the working men, to whom we wish to extend the franchise, bestir themselves and enable us to help them to it'.[272] John Snowden, by this time a forty-year-old man, was an early member of this Association.

As a young man, he had been arrested in the cause of a vote for the people. His journey in an omnibus down Salterhebble Hill had caused a riot. He had been regarded by the Halifax authorities as a dangerous activist and he had eventually suffered a spell in the Halifax workhouse in 1856 after Edward Akroyd introduced machinery which, finally, put an end to the independent hand combers of Halifax.[273] Now, in 1866, he and Halifax mill-owner Robert Crossley, of Arden House, travelled together in the first week of February, as delegates of the Halifax Parliamentary Reform Association to meet and lobby the liberal Whig prime minister, Lord John Russell, for extended (not the Chartists' universal) voting rights. They were met there by Francis Crossley, parliamentary member for the West Riding of Yorkshire, who told them the prime minister was willing to receive a deputation of four working men. 'I proposed our ... esteemed Snowden as one of the four', says Robert Crossley, who respected his companion for his 'calm and thoughtful resource in all emergencies when engaged in the discharge of any public duty of this kind'.[274]

'My Lord', said Snowden to Russell on 8th February 1866, "I am one of the working class who believe that the theory of our Government is founded upon the principle of supposition that all classes of Her Majesty's subjects are alike entitled to representation in the House of Commons; and as the Reform Act of 1832, of which your Lordship was the author, only enfranchised the middle or trading classes, leaving the working classes entirely without the pale, they desire, after so many years have elapsed, to be admitted now at least to a reasonable share in the representation". As it happens, the Liberal Russell government would not be the one to bring in a Reform Bill, although it tried.

British governments, of whatever hue, were expert at ignoring dissent whenever they could, crushing it when they needed to, applying brutal punishment on the one hand and pragmatic leniency on the other. It is interesting to find John Frost lecturing on the 'Horrors of Transportation' at Halifax in October 1857, nearly twenty years after he had been condemned to death by hanging for leading the attack on Newport. His commuted sentence to life transportation had been lifted and he was allowed to return home. Benjamin Wilson says of their meeting, 'If someone had said to me when John Frost was transported for life for riots in 1839 that I should meet and shake hands with him, I should have come to the conclusion that I would have to be in Van-Diemen's Land'.[275] British governments gave way to political demands on their own terms in small, incremental steps, by which they managed to let off the steam of public pressure and keep the lid on the boiler.

A speech which gives a good example of the philosophy which allowed this slow change was made in 1850, when the danger of revolution in England had been effectively dealt with. Lord Palmerston, who had supported Lord Ashley during his fight for the Mines and Collieries Regulation Act, addressed the House of Commons on 25th June 1850: "We have shown the example of a nation, in which every class of society accepts with cheerfulness the lot which Providence has assigned to it; while at the same time every individual of each class is constantly striving to raise himself in the social scale ... by persevering good conduct, and by the steady and energetic exertion of the moral and intellectual faculties with which his Creator has endowed him. To govern such a people as this, is indeed an object worthy of the ambition of the noblest man who lives in the land",[276] and by this, the idea, even the propriety, that social inequalities were not set in concrete but were removable was placed in the nation's consciousness. At the time of this conciliatory speech, Ernest Jones was still in prison.

The panacea of self-help, this 'constant striving to raise' oneself within the set order, was alluringly romantic and powerful, it carried a strong momentum, and it appealed to many working men like John Snowden. It was a notion which sat comfortably with the lost perfection of artisan self-sufficiency, those 'lusty self-employed fellows' who had been destroyed by the processes of industrialisation. It is in the light of all this that John Snowden joined the middle-class movement for political and social reform while the probability of an extended vote grew politically attractive in the corridors of power. After more demonstrations, this time in London and Birmingham, wondrously, after all the years of effort and fighting, a Second Reform Act was passed. The Reform Act of 1867 doubled voting numbers across the country. The electorate in Halifax rose from less than two thousand to some nine thousand.[277]

That was in 1867. John Snowden died at Halifax in 1884. Not long before, he said that he 'anticipated that before the present Parliament comes to an end a bill would be enacted making every householder an enfranchised citizen'. And indeed, another Reform Act in 1884 gave nearly half the male population the vote. But the Chartists' universal male franchise still was not won. The remainder of men and every woman would have to wait until after the First World War for their voting rights. In 1842 working women appear to have accepted that to possess the vote through their husbands would be a great thing, and they had marched side-by-side with men for this principle.[*] To be politically represented as a class, to be able to vote away 'white slavery', was what mattered. Women would have to fight all over again for their individual right to vote, but all men were represented in full, at last, by 1918.

John Snowden died, just days before the passing of the 1884

---

[*]   A National Society of Women's Suffrage was founded in 1867.

Reform Act, at his home at 29 Portland Road, Range Bank, the road above New Bank where the military, the special constables and the magistrates had confronted the great mass of Bradford marchers on 15th August 1842; the road which overlooks the place where the 11th Hussars, the 61st of Foot and the inhabitants of Halifax met so violently on Tuesday 16th August 1842, when so many were injured or lost their lives. Now Range Bank and North Bridge were thronged with those come to pay their respects to an old Chartist as his coffin of pitch pine was taken along the way to Northgate-end chapel, on the afternoon of Thursday 11th September 1884. John Snowden had learned to write only twenty years earlier but had read his constitutional history thoroughly. It had been his 'somewhat whimsical method', said Rev. F. M Millsen in the chapel, 'to put himself in a very humble place, and when he rose to speak he would apologise for offering his advice. You well know how he did it, but he never rose till things were getting hazy or we were drifting into some dangerous or impractical policy, and then his thorough knowledge of his subject and his devotion to the cause were manifest'.[278]

At the service were his family, men and women just come from their places of work and, significantly, many members of Halifax's industry-owning families. On leaving the chapel, those come to mark his passing were watched by a great crowd which had gathered along Northgate, and as the cortege went along Broad Street and Corporation Street at the start of its procession to Illingworth Church, many more Halifax people came out of their homes to show their respect. And so ends the story of Chartism, at Halifax and elsewhere, which, surely so far as John Snowden was concerned, was a success story.

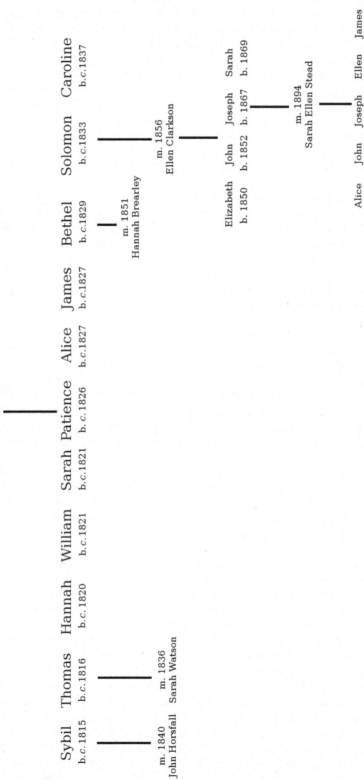

John & Elizabeth Kershaw

Sybil b.c.1815 · Thomas b.c.1816 · Hannah b.c.1820 · William b.c.1821 · Sarah b.c.1821 · Patience b.c.1826 · Alice b.c.1827 · James b.c.1827 · Bethel b.c.1829 · Solomon b.c.1833 · Caroline b.c.1837

Sybil — m. 1840 John Horsfall
Thomas — m. 1836 Sarah Watson

Bethel — m. 1851 Hannah Brearley

Solomon — m. 1856 Ellen Clarkson

Elizabeth b. 1850 · John b. 1852 · Joseph b. 1867 · Sarah b. 1869

John — m. 1894 Sarah Ellen Stead

Alice b. 1897 · John b. 1900 · Joseph b. 1902 · Ellen b. 1904 · James b. 1911

18

Patience

And so the Mines and Collieries Regulation Act was passed; the Ten Hours Act was passed; the Reform Acts of 1867 and 1884 were passed. The passing of these Acts did not necessarily mean things got better for industrial workers. In the mills, increased mechanisation brought greater operational pressures to the mainly child and female workforce. As to social abuses, at Calvert's mill, isolated high up at Wainstalls above the source of the Hebble Brook, orphan children continued to be used for decades more and were paid pocket money for a fifty-six hour week.[279] For the miners, things tended to get harder because, as the years passed, it became necessary to dig deeper and deeper to find new seams.[280]

Even so, long after the time of its passing into law, many believed the Mines and Collieries Regulation Act of 1842 to be 'probably the most revolutionary piece of industrial legislation ever placed on Britain's Statue Book'.[281] It was possibly the first piece of legislation which really made industrialists adapt their ways to that of a greater will. It certainly affected the lives of women and children like Patience Kershaw. There can be little as bad as spending twelve hours and more each day pushing heavy wood and iron corves loaded with coal through pitch dark, sharp, wet, low tunnels; being hit and abused by your fellow workers; having no education, your body ruined, your mind stunned, your spirit wrung dry. At the very least, twenty-eight children died in the Halifax, Huddersfield and Low Moor coal mines between 1838 and 1841 and many more were abused and made unutterably miserable.[282] Had Lord Ashley, brought into the fray by Richard Oastler, not pressed for a Commission in 1841 to look beyond child employment in the textile trades, Patience Kershaw would have continued this work long beyond her seventeenth birthday and a new generation of infants drawn in.

By 1851 Patience, now a young woman of twenty-six, was working as a woolcomber at Upper Popples in Northowram, lodging there with a thirty-year old man called William Horsfall. William also was a woolcomber and, in all probability, had taught Patience the skill. Life would be hard for them because combers were on strike against wage reductions at this time. The national census enumerators' books give a ten yearly insight into private lives. In the years between each census there is no way to know much of what Patience did, where she lived, whom she met or what she thought, but here at least is confirmation that when the work at Joseph Stocks' Boothtown Colliery ended in 1842, she went on to learn the skill of woolcombing and, in 1851, was working alongside William Horsfall. Her eldest sister, Sybil, was working as a power loom weaver and living with her husband, John Horsfall, over the hill in the village of Northowram. And on Christmas Day, 1851, there was a family event when their younger brother Bethel, now a twenty-four-year-old fully-fledged miner and living at Clayton, married Hannah Briearly at Halifax Parish Church.

Of Patience's sisters Sarah, Alice and Caroline, no trace is found beyond their census entry made at the terraces on Plough Croft Lane in 1841 and Patience's mention of them to Samuel Scriven in that year. No marriage, no death. Also the family of Patience's eldest brother Thomas Kershaw, his wife Sarah Watson and their two daughters, disappears after 1841. Her second-eldest brother William, a twenty-year-old miner in 1841, is not to be found in any of the census enumerators' books after this decade, and no marriage or death has been found.

After his Christmas Day marriage in 1851, Patience's brother Bethel and wife Hannah, moved to Leeds. Their children were born there. Bethel's younger brother, Solomon, followed him to Leeds, having also progressed from Boothtown hurrier to miner, and in 1856 he married a Leeds woman called Ellen Clarkson. Ellen came from a weaver's family. She and Solomon had a son and a daughter who were given the names of their Kershaw grandparents, John and Elizabeth, and later another boy called Joseph. Patience's two brothers lived close by each other, Bethel on Windsor Street in the parish of St Stephen's, Solomon on Apple Street.

Their lives certainly were different from their father's, John Kershaw. Bethel and Solomon married their partners and their children were likely to have learned to read and write. This generation seems to be emerging from the cocoon of stoical existence which surrounded the lives of the mining families of Northowram in previous generations. And in all likelihood Bethel and Solomon would be members of a local miners' union.

The Miners' Association of Great Britain and Ireland, set-up in the focal year of 1842, lasted until the late 1840s when it met its gradual demise, at which local unions served in its place. From its ashes rose the National Miners' Association of the 1850s, and its ghost smiled upon the Miners' Federation of Great Britain of 1888. From the Federation came The National Union of Mineworkers, founded on 1st January 1945. Throughout most of the 1840s the Miners' Association of Great Britain and Ireland successfully fought threatening legislation, worked for increased safety measures, wages and for better working terms. Perhaps, above all, it gave legal protection to its members through the work of lawyer W. P. Roberts which was a remarkable departure for organisations of its kind at this time. W. P. Roberts' work made it harder for the mine owners to get round the provisions of the 1842 Mines and Collieries Regulation Act, as so many mill owners had got round the Factory Act of 1833.

That the Association, still Yorkshire based, was intended as a British body is another significant departure from earlier union practice and a status it found hard to attain. No matter the encouragement, throughout the autumn months of 1842 other miners' associations would not respond to the Association's calls to combine. On 31st December 1842, four months after its inaugural meeting at Wakefield, the Association, in desperation, placed an article in the *Northern Star* appealing to miners beyond Yorkshire to make contact. 'Fellow Workmen', it began, 'boldly come forward and assert your rights ... there is no power on earth can prevent you from being paid for your labour, if you will only be true to yourselves.'

> What would England have been but for the colliers? Would it have been
> the manufacturer of the world? ... Let us make one simultaneous effort
> to throw off our present yoke of oppression ... We request that the men

of every pit will appoint a man to write, or forward to us, addressed to the Colliers, Griffin Inn, Wakefield, every accident, and all information concerning the miseries that oppress you; those facts carefully collected and printed, will show to the world such a picture as it never saw before.[283]

Miners everywhere knew there were details to be revealed beyond even those uncovered by Lord Ashley's commissioners of 1841. Between 1841 and 1849, newspapers reported eight major pit disasters within Yorkshire's borders alone in which more than two hundred men and eighty children were killed. Then there were all the many individual incidents which never made their way into the national, or even local press as well as the hundreds of early deaths from lung disease which remained publicly obscure. The same story was, of course, repeated in Durham, Lancashire, the Midlands, Wales, and Scotland. It is reported that, in the year 1869 alone, there were more than eleven hundred deaths in the mines, which means that, on a yearly basis, one out of every three hundred miners, man and child, was losing his life through accident.[284] And in 1869, as in 1842, the feeling remained that 'the sufferers are, in the great majority of instances, to blame'. 'Accidents, as they are called ... arise from the gross, heedless, devil-daring obstinacy of the miners'.[285] There was still no regulation of working practices in the mines, no owner responsibility.

The *Northern Star* column brought an initial response to the Association's 1842 appeal from miners at Cowpen, Cramlington and Seaton, and a national association was in the making.[286] The Miners' Association of Great Britain and Ireland brought its members out from a dark place and from isolation, and into a world in which they might make their way with some confidence. Lord Ashley's Mines and Collieries Regulation Act of 1842, which resulted from the work of sub-commissioner Samuel Scriven and his colleagues, had been a trigger to the creation of the Miners' Association of Great Britain and Ireland; the appearance of the miners on the streets of Halifax on 1st August 1842 a signal of changes to come.

It is not possible to know what happened to Patience during the 1850s but the 1861 census shows that, by then, she had left William Horsfall's house and was living beside the Illingworth road at Ovenden. She is listed in the census enumerator's book as a servant in the house of a weaver, Henry Shaw, a forty-two-year-old widower and his daughters, eleven-year-old Sarah, a worsted spinner, and Betty, just five. Patience left Henry Shaw's household in the early 1860s and within a handful of years some unknown but insurmountable trouble overtook her which brought her to the Halifax workhouse on Gibbet Street; the place which once had been called a Bastille. Patience is described as a washerwoman. She would be working in the workhouse laundry.

It is now that Patience began to show signs of mental disturbance. She was still living at the Halifax workhouse in 1867, the exciting year of the Reform Act which extended voting rights, but for Patience 1867 was a year when she was likely to strike-out violently and when she was finding difficulty in speaking properly. Her strong legs were no longer strong. She had begun to shuffle when walking. Because of these symptoms, she was taken from Halifax workhouse to the Stanley Road Lunatic Asylum just outside Wakefield, in the last month of 1867. Samuel Tuke had been consulted on the building of the asylum and it ran on the principles of well supervised and compassionate treatment.

Patience had lost contact with her brothers Bethel and Solomon over in Leeds, and with her sister Sybil, now widowed and living at Northowram. In answer to her medical report query, 'Name and residence of nearest known relative', 'None' was written. But she remembered a Jack who, she thought, was still coming into her room at night with his dogs. She received a thorough medical examination at Stanley. None there would know of her childhood years as a hurrier down Boothtown Colliery but they noted, as Samuel Scriven had, that she was below average height. Patience, in 1867, seemed to be in pretty good physical condition but her speech was 'tremulous and hesitating' and 'she drags her limbs in walk'. Also, her pupils were equally dilated. Her appetite, though, was good.[287]

Patience grew more and more incapacitated. At the beginning of

March 1869 she 'began to sink, and sank rapidly', so that by Friday 12th March, '[h]er mind', wrote her attendant, 'is perfectly gone'. Patience died that day, fifteen months after arriving at Stanley asylum, of general paralysis of the insane. General paralysis of the insane is strongly associated with untreated syphilis. Patience was described insane because it seems, through an affliction passed to her by a careless or unwitting sexual partner, her brain had suffered physical damage. She lived for just forty-two years. One other name appears on Patience's death certificate, that of James Crichton Browne, who added his signature to the document as the registrar's informant. James Crichton Browne was the medical officer appointed to the asylum, a man who pursued scientific enlightenment, corresponded with Charles Darwin, and who considered himself, 'the guardian and friend as well as the medical adviser of his patients'.[288] He was responsible for Patience during her last days and seems to have been a man possessed of some compassion.

The last we see of this generation of coal-mining Kershaws is two years later. Solomon in 1871, and now thirty-eight years old, is living on Windsor Street, in Leeds. His brother Bethel had died just before Christmas the year before, of bronchitis, and Solomon, by then suffering from the same condition brought on by breathing-in coal dust for more than thirty years, continued to work down a Leeds' pit. His first born son, John, thirteen years old, like so many of his forebears, male and female, was working as a hurrier.

Postscript

No story has an ending. Patience Kershaw's brother, Solomon died when just thirty-nine years old, fourteen months after his brother Bethel, in February 1872, of lung disease. His son John, now fourteen years old, continued as a hurrier after his father's death and grew to be a miner in his own right. John lived with his sister and mother right through to the early 1900s in Leeds while his brother, Joseph, worked as an iron foundry core maker. Joseph's four surviving children, the great-grandchildren of John and Elizabeth Kershaw of Boothtown, the great-nieces and great-nephews of Patience Kershaw, were born in the early 1900s.

Not one of these children worked in a mine or factory during their infancy and early childhood, all went to school. And Patience's descendants, wherever they may be, today enjoy an unfettered right to vote for a parliamentary representative.

Bibliography

PRIMARY SOURCES

Reports

First Report of the Children's Employment Commission (Mines) 1842. The original
document is not available at the National Archives. According to Ian
Winstanley, it was sold into private hands in the 1990s. To my knowledge, Ian
Winstanley's online transcription through The Coal Mining History Resource
Centre, Picks Publishing, is the only available source and the one used here. I
have cited page numbers relating to Mr. Winstanley's transcription wherever
possible.

HO 40/59 : *Report to Members of the Manufacturers' Relief Committee (dated
February 1843)*. Held at the National Archives, Kew

HO 45/264 : Comprising letters to the Home Office relating to the disturbances.
Held at the National Archives, Kew

HO 45/265-6-7-8 : Chartism, Ireland, Public Disorder, Migration, Labour. Held at
the National Archives, Kew

Stanley Road Hospital medical case book records C85/3/6/20/p333A-333B/1. Held
at Wakefield Archives

TS 11/814 2678 : Crime, Treason and Rebellion, Public Disorder. Held at the
National Archives, Kew

WO 12/1005 : 11th Hussars Records created or inherited by the War Office,
Armed Forces, Judge Advocate General, and related bodies 1841-43. Held at
the National Archives, Kew

Letters

VIN 1/1/1-10 Henry Vincent held at the Labour History Archive, Manchester

Newspapers

Bradford Observer and Halifax, Huddersfield, and Keighley Reporter (held at
Halifax Reference Library)

Halifax and Huddersfield Express (held at Halifax Reference Library)

Halifax Courier (held at Halifax Reference Library)

Halifax Guardian and Huddersfield and Bradford Advertiser (held at Halifax Reference Library)

Leeds Mercury (held at Leeds Archives)

Manchester Guardian (on line at Gale Group)

Monmouth Merlin (held at Newtown Archives)

Northern Star (online at Gale Group)

Maps

held at Halifax Reference Library:

1842 Rawson, Charles: Plan of the Borough of Halifax: 912:42

RAW 1847 Halifax (County Series)

HT:19A 1827 Days Plan

HT15

Publications

BATES, JOHN, *John Bates, the veteran Reformer: a sketch of his life,* held at Bradford Local Studies (B920 BAT)

BROUGH, BARNABAS, 'A Night with the Chartists, Frost, Williams and Jones', W.M. Clark, London (held at Newport Reference Library M160 342 BRO)

COOPER, THOMAS, Life of Thomas Cooper, Leicester University Press ([1872], 1971 edition).

CRABTREE, G., *A Brief Description of a Tour Through Calder Dale*, Huddersfield printed by J. Hobson, (1833).

CRABTREE, JOHN, *Concise History of the Parish and Vicarage of Halifax*, Hartley and Walker, (1836).
online facsimile – https://archive.org/details/concisehistoryof00crab

CRICHTON BROWNE, J., *The West Riding Lunatic Asylum Medical Reports*, J & A Churchill, London, (1871).
online facsimile – https://archive.org/details/39002086346294.med.yale.edu

ENGELS, F., *Condition of the Working Classes in England,* Oxford University Press, (1845).

GAMMAGE, ROBERT GEORGE, *History of the Chartist Movement 1837-1854*, Newcastle-on-Tyne, Browne & Browne, Forgotten Books ([1894], 2012 edition).

GRUNDY, FRANCIS H., *Pictures of the Past: Memories of Men I have Met and Places I have Seen*, Griffith and Farran, (1879, Bibliolife facsimile)

GURNEY, JOSEPH AND THOMAS, *The Trial of John Frost*, printed by Luke G. and Luke J. Hansard, London, (1840), held at Newport Reference Library.

HARWOOD, H. W., in MULROY, *Story of the Town that Bred Us*, held at Halifax Reference Library (Ref: 942.746 MUL).

HOLYOAKE, G. J., *The History of Co-operation in Halifax*, London Book Store.

JOHNS, W. N., 'Chartist Riots at Newport MS', (1889), held at Newport Reference Library M160 342 JOH.

LAWSON, J., *Letters to the Young on Progress in Pudsey during the Last Sixty Years*. Stanningley, J. W. Birdsall, (1887), held at Halifax Reference Library 942.746 LAW.

OASTLER, RICHARD, *The Fleet Papers; being letters to Thomas Thornhill, Esq.*, Vol II, W. J. Cleaver, (1842),
online facsimile – https://archive.org/details/fleetpapersbeing02grah

O'CONNOR, FERGUS, *The Trial of Feargus O'Connor, Barrister-at-Law, and fifty-eight others at Lancaster*, Forgotten Book facsimile ([1843], 2012 edition).

OWEN, ROBERT, *Life of Robert Owen, by himself*, Charles Knight & Co Ltd, (1857).

PEEL, FRANK, *Rising of the Luddites, Chartists and Plug-Drawers*, Frank Cass & Co Ltd, (1880).

RANGER, WILLIAM, *Report to the General Board of Health, on a preliminary inquiry as to the sewerage, drainage, and supply of water, and the sanitary conditions of the inhabitants of the town of Halifax in the County of York, by W. Ranger, Superintendant Inspector 1851*, (1851), held at Halifax Reference Library, Ref. 352.6 RAN.

Stanley Road Hospital medical case book records, held at Wakefield Archives, Ref. C85/3/6/20/p333A-333B/1.

Walkers' Directory of the Parish of Halifax 1845, Ryburn Archive Edition, (1991).

WILSON, BENJAMIN, *Struggles of an Old Chartist*, (1887), held at Halifax Reference Library 942.081).

SECONDARY SOURCES

Publications

BEST, GEOFFREY, *Mid-Victorian Britain 1851-75*, Fontana Press, (1971).

BLACK, DAVID & CHRIS FORD, *1839: The Chartist Insurrection*, Unkant London, (2012).

BRIGGS, ASA, *Chartist Studies*, Macmillan St Martin's Press, (1959).

_____, *A Social History of England*, Book Club Associates by arrangement with Weidenfield and Nicolson, (1984).

CHALLINOR, RAYMOND & BRIAN RIPLEY, *The Miners' Association – A Trade Union in the Age of the Chartists*, Lawrence and Wishart, London, (1968).

CHAMBERS, J. D., *The Workshop of the World*, Oxford University Press, (1968).

CLAYRE, ALASDAIR, *Nature and Industrialization*, Oxford University Press in association with The Open University, (1977)

COLE, G. D. H., *Chartist Portraits*, Cassell History, (1941).

COLE, G. D. H. AND FILSON, A. W., *British Working Class Movements, Selected Documents 1789-1875*, Macmillan & Co Ltd

COURT, W. H. B., *A Concise Economic History of Britain*, Cambridge University Press, (1967).

CROSS, SIMON J., 'Owenite Socialism and anti-Socialism in Halifax 1829-1945', in *Halifax Antiquarian Society*, (2007).

DALBY, G. R., 'The Chartist Movement in Halifax District 1848', in *Halifax Antiquarian Society*, (1956).

EDSALL, NICHOLAS C., *The Anti-Poor Law Movement 1834-44* , Manchester University Press, (1971).

EPSTEIN, JAMES, *The Lion of Freedom*, Croom Helm Ltd, (1982).

EPSTEIN, JAMES & DOROTHY THOMPSON, (eds.), *The Chartist Experience, Studies of Working Class Radicalism and Culture 1830-1860*, Macmillan Press Ltd, (1982).

FINN, MARGOT C., *After Chartism: Class and Nation in English Radical Politics 1848-1874*, Cambridge University Press, (1993).

FOOT, PAUL, *The Vote, How It was Won and How It was Undermined*, Viking an imprint of Penguin Books, (2005).

GREGG, PAULINE, *A Social and Economic History of Britain 1760-1980*, Harrap, (1982).

HAMISH FRASER, J., *Trade Unions and Society, The Struggle for Acceptance, 1850-1880*, George Allen and Unwin, (1974).

HAMISH FRASER, J., *A History of British Trade Unionism 1700-1998*, Macmillan Press Ltd, (1999).

HAMMOND, J. L. AND B. HAMMOND, *The Skilled Labourer 1760-1832*, Alan Sutton Publishing Ltd, (1995).

HAMPTON, C. (ed), *A Radical Reader, The Struggle for Change in England 1381-1914*, Penguin, (1984).

HANSON, T. W., *The Story of Halifax*, Halifax, F. King & Sons, (1920).

HARGREAVES, JOHN A., *Benjamin Rushton, Handloom Weaver and Chartist*, Screeve for The Friends of the Lister Lane Cemetery, (2006).

HOLROYD, J., 'Textile Mills, Masters and Men in the Halifax District 1770-1851', in *Halifax Antiquarian Society*, (1979).

INGRAMS, RICHARD, *The Life and Adventures of William Cobbett*, Harper Perennial, (2005).

IWAMA, TOSHIHIKO, *Middle class in Halifax 1780-1850*, University of Leeds, (2003). Thesis held at Halifax Reference Library.

JENKINS, MICK, *The General Strike of 1842*, Lawrence and Wishart, (1980).

JONES, DAVID J. V., *The Last Rising, The Newport Insurrection of 1839*, Clarendon Press, (1985).

JOWITT, J. A., 'Parliamentary Politics in Halifax 1823-1847', *Northern History*, Vol XII (1976).

MULROY, J. J., *Story of the Town that Bred Us*, (1948), held a Halifax Reference Library (Ref: 942.746 MUL).

MUSSON, A. E., *Trade Union and Social History*, Frank Cass: London, (1974).

NORMAN, ANDREW, *The Story of George Loveless and the Tolpuddle Martyrs*, Halsgrove, (2008).

RIDD, T., 'Hurriers and Thrusters', in *Halifax Antiquarian Society* (1966).

ONSLOW GARNETT, W., *A History of I & I Calvert Ltd., of Wainstalls Mills,1821-1951*, (1951), available at: From Weaver to Web online visual archive of Calderdale History

PEACOCK, A. J. , 'Bradford Chartism 1838-1840' St Anthony's Press, York (Borthwick Institute of Historical Research No. 36), (1969).

PEEL, FRANK, *Spen Valley: Past and Present*, Kirklees Leisure Services, (1987).

SPENCER, COLIN, 'Township Workhouse', in *Halifax Antiquarian Society*, (1983).

TAWNEY, R. H., *Religion and the Rise of Capitalism*, Pelican ([1926], 1961 editon)

THOMPSON, DOROTHY, *The Early Chartists*, Macmillan, (1971).

_____, *The Chartists: Popular Politics in the Industrial Revolution*, Wildwood House, (1986), *reprinted* Breviary Stuff Publications, (2013).

THOMPSON, DOROTHY & THOMPSON, E. P., 'Halifax as a Chartist Centre', unpublished essay held at Halifax Reference Library (Ref: 942.081 THO).

THOMPSON, E. P., *The Making of the English Working Class*, Pantheon Books, New York, (1964).

TILLER, KATE, 'Late Chartism: Halifax 1847-58' in EPSTEIN, JAMES & THOMPSON, DOROTHY (eds.) *The Chartist Experience: Studies in Working-Class Radicalism and Culture*, 1830–1860 , London, (1982).

Trade Unions in the Victorian Age, Volume I, 1823-1834, Gregg International Publishers Limited, Victorian Social Conscience series, (1973).

TRIGG, W. B., 'The Halifax Coalfield', in *Halifax Antiquarian Society*, (1986).

WARD, J. T., *The Factory Movement 1830-1855*, Macmillan & Co. Ltd, (1962).

WASHINGTON, J. G., 'Poverty Health & Social Welfare, the history of Halifax Union Workhouse and St John's 1834-1972', in *Halifax Antiquarian Society*, (1997).

WEBSTER, ERIC, 'The Halifax Guardian and Halifax Courier', in *Halifax Antiquarian Society*, (1996).

_____, 'Edward Akroyd (1810-1887) also a brief history of James Akroyd & Son', in *Halifax Antiquarian Society*, (1987).

WESLEY BREADY, J., *Lord Shaftesbury and Social-Industrial Progress*, George Allen & Unwin Ltd, (1926).

WILD, J., 'Halifax Railway Station', in *Halifax Antiquarian Society*, (1968).

NOTES

1 Daniel Defoe, *A Tour through the whole island of Great Britain*, in Clayre, p. 3.

2 *The Leeds Mercury*, Saturday, July 7, 1838.

3 *First Report of the Children's Employment Commission (Mines) 1842*, p. 1.

4 *First Report of the Children's Employment Commission (Mines) 1842.*

5 *First Report of the Children's Employment Commission (Mines) 1842.*

6 Machinery comprised either a hand-winch, sometimes operated by a woman or a youngster, or a horse-gin, where a young boy or girl walked a horse round in a circle for leverage.

7 *First Report of the Children's Employment Commission (Mines) 1842*, p. 6.

8 *First Report of the Children's Employment Commission (Mines) 1842*, p. 19.

9 Hanson, T. W. (1920) p. 186.

10 For a description of Halifax at this time Crabtree, G. (1833), p. 3 and Crabtree, John (1836), p. 308.

11 Wesley Bready (1926), p. 185.

12 Crabtree, G. (1833), p. 23.

13 Wesley Bready (1926), p. 187.

14 Wesley Bready (1926), p. 228.

15 Wesley Bready (1926), p. 188.

16 *Halifax Guardian*, June 11, 1842, p. 2.

17 *Halifax Guardian*, June 11, 1842, p. 2.

18 Grundy, F. (1879), pp. 99-100.

19 Hanson, T. W. (1920), p. 259.

20 Hanson, T. W. (1920), p. 231.

21 Trigg, W. B. p. 82.

22 Crabtree, John (1836), table p. 313.

23 1841 census and Walker's Directory.

24 Holroyd, J. (1979), p. 60.

25 Thompson, D. (1986), p. 350.

26 Queenshead is now considered part of Queensbury.

27 *Northern Star* 8 August 1846.

28 O'Connor (1843), p. vii.

29 Crabtree, G (1833), pp. 12-14, 17-20, and Fielden, J. (1836), pp. 5-6.

30 Cole, G. D.H. & A. W. Filson pp. 334-5.

31 *Walkers Directory.*

32 *The Sheffield Independent and Yorkshire and Derbyshire Advertiser*, Saturday, May 20, 1837.

33 *The Morning Post* (London) Friday, May 19, 1837, p. 7; *Preston Chronicle*, Saturday, May 27 1837.

NOTES

34   Cooper, Thomas, pp. 157-8.

35   Black, D. and C. Ford, p. 17.

36   Iwama, T, p. 167.

37   *Northern Star and Leeds General Advertiser*, Saturday, January 6, 1838.

38   Bates, John (1895), no pagination.

39   *Northern Star and Leeds General Advertiser*, Saturday, January 27, 1838; I have reverted the tense of this report to the present.

40   Evidence given to the Police Commission of 1836 in Thompson, D. (1986), p. 244.

41   Gammage, R. G. (1894), p. 94.

42   Gammage, R. G. (1894), p. 95.

43   VIN 1/1/10.

44   Thompson, D & E. P., unpublished, p. 21.

45   *The Charter*, 5 May 1839, p. 229.

46   *The London Democrat* (1839), in Cole, G. D. H. (1941), p. 276.

47   *Northern Star,* Jan 19 1839.

48   *People's Paper* 14 July 1852, in Hampton, C. (1984) p. 515. See also Tawney, R. H. (1926) pp. 103-4 for an excellent discussion on religion and capitalism.

49   Wilson, B. (1887), p. 1.

50   Wilson, B. (1887), p. 3.

51   *Bradford Observer* May 23 1839, p. 3 cols. 4- 6.

52   Gammage, R. G. (1894) p. 83.

53   *Bradford Observer*, May 23 1839, p. 3. col. 2.

54   *Northern Star*, 8 Dec 1838, p. 4 col. 1.

55   See Thompson, D. (1971) p. 226.

56   In Peacock, A. J. (1969) pp. 24, 28.

57   In Thompson, D & E. P., unpublished, p. 24.

58   VIN 1/1/10.

59   In Jones, D. J. V. (1985), p. 73.

60   In Black, D. & C. Ford (2012), p. 91.

61   *Northern Star*, 6 April 1839, p. 6, col. 2.

62   Holyoake, G. J. (1893), Vol. 1, pp. 83-4.

63   *Northern Star*, Saturday, August 17, 1839.

64   Peacock, A. J. (1969), pp. 22-3.

65   *Northern Star,* Saturday, August 17, 1839.

66   *Northern Star*, Saturday, August 31, 1839.

67   Peel, F. (1880), p. 313.

68   *Northern Star* 5 Oct 1839, p. 6, col. 2.

69   See Jones, D. J. V. (1985) for the full story of the attack upon Newport.

70   O'Connor, F. (1843), p. 417.

71 Thompson, D. (1971), p. 228; Peacock, A. J. (1969), p. 32.

72 Dr William Price in Jones, D. J. V. (1985), pp. 101-2, taken from the *Cardiff Times* 26 May 1888.

73 Black, D. & C. Ford (2012), p. 123.

74 Brough, B., p. 11.

75 Brough, B., pp. 11, 12. Also *Monmouthshire Merlin*, Nov 9 1839, p. 4, col. 1; and eye-witness, Thomas Bevan Oliver, in Gurney, J. & T. (1840), p. 214.

76 In Gammage, R. G. (1894), p. 163.

77 Gurney, J. & T. (1840), p. 216.

78 Jones, D. J. V. (1985), p. 33.

79 *Bradford Observer*, Thursday, November 7, 1839.

80 In Thompson, D. & E. P. (unpublished), p. 30.

81 *Halifax Courier*, September 6, 1884, p. 7.

82 In Peacock, A. J. (1969), p. 24.

83 In Peacock, A. J. (1969), p. 33.

84 In Dalby, G. R., pp. 109-10.

85 TS 11/814 2680 (209-210).

86 In Thompson, D. (1971), p. 208.

87 See Thompson, D. (1971), pp. 209-10.

88 Ranger, W. (1851), p. 102.

89 Ranger, W. (1851), pp. 46-8.

90 In Thompson, D. & E. P. (unpublished), p. 25.

91 See Thompson, D. (1971), p. 284.

92 Samuel Foxhall, in Thompson, D. (1971), p. 264.

93 James Harrison, in Thompson, D. (1971), p. 280.

94 *Halifax Courier*, 6 Sept 1884, p. 7.

95 *Sheffield & Rotherham Independent*, Saturday, January 18, 1840, p. 7.

96 *Halifax Guardian*, Jan 18, 1840.

97 TS 11/814 (2680) and *Sheffield & Rotherham Independent*, 18 January, 1840.

98 *Halifax Guardian*, Jan 18, 1840.

99 *Halifax Express*, Jan 25 p. 3.

100 TS 11/814 2678 (26).

101 TS 11/814 2680 (21).

102 TS 11/814 2678 (25).

103 TS 11/814 2680 (9).

104 TS 11/814 2678 (24).

105 TS 11/814 2680 (8) for numbers of weaponry.

106 *Halifax Guardian*, Feb 2, 1840.

107 *Northern Star*, Saturday, July 20, 1839; p. 8, col. 5.

NOTES

108 Owen, R. (1857), pp. 104-5.

109 Thompson, D. (1986), p. 283.

110 *Halifax Express*, Jan 4 1840, p. 2.

111 *First Report of the Children's Employment Commission (Mines) 1842.*

112 *First Report of the Children's Employment Commission (Mines) 1842*, p. 2.

113 Seymour Tremenheere 1844 Commission to Scotland taken from the Coal Mining History Resource Centre, Picks Publishing and Ian Winstanley.

114 See Crabtree, J. (1836) tables; and *Walker's Trade Directory.*

115 *First Report of the Children's Employment Commission (Mines) 1842.* p. 11.

116 All quotations from Samuel Scriven are taken from Ian Winstanley's online transcription of the *First Report of the Children's Employment Commission (Mines) 1842.*

117 Engels, 1845, p. 253.

118 *First Report of the Children's Employment Commission (Mines) 1842.*

119 *First Report of the Children's Employment Commission (Mines) 1842.*

120 Wilson, B. (1887), p. 4.

121 *Halifax Guardian*, July 8, 1841.

122 Gammage, R. G. (1894), pp. 216-17.

123 *Northern Star*, 4 Dec 1841 p. 1.

124 Oastler, R, (1842), Vol II, p. 1.

125 O'Connor, F. (1843), p. 249.

126 Richard Pilling in O'Connor, F. (1843), p. 243.

127 *Halifax Guardian*, Feb 26, 1842 and March 3, 1842.

128 Gammage, R. G. (1894), p. 209.

129 Webster, E., pp. 60-1.

130 *Halifax Guardian*, May 14 1842, p. 4, col. 3.

131 *Halifax Guardian*, May 21 1842, p. 4.

132 *First Report of the Children's Employment Commission (Mines) 1842*, p. 20.

133 *Sheffield & Rotherham Independent*, Saturday, January 18, 1840, p. 2.

134 In Thompson, D. (1971), p. 281.

135 *Halifax Guardian*, July 16 1842.

136 Wesley Bready, J. (1926), p. 290.

137 P. Ainsworth, in Wesley Bready, J. (1926), p. 299.

138 Wesley Bready, J. (1926), p. 303.

139 *Halifax Guardian,* Aug 6 1842, p. 5.

140 *Bradford Observer and Halifax, Huddersfield, and Keighley Reporter*, Thursday, August 4, 1842 p.1, col. 5.

141 Oastler, R. (1842) Vol II, p. 211.

142 See Thompson, D. (1986), pp. 277-8.

143 *Leeds Mercury*, 6 Aug 1842, p. 4, col. 3; *Halifax Guardian*, 6 Aug 1842, p. 5.

144 Strikes took place in Cornwall up to Scotland, in Suffolk across to Wales, the vast majority occurring in Lancashire and Yorkshire, (see Jenkins, M. (1980), p. 188).

145 See O'Connor.F (1843), pp. 25, 40.

146 Daniel Maude, Manchester magistrate, letter to the *Guardian*, in Jenkins, M. (1980), p. 77.

147 O'Connor, F. (1843), p. 420.

148 In Jenkins, M. (1980), p. 167.

149 O'Connor, F. (1843), p. 7.

150 *Manchester Times and Gazette*, Saturday, August 20, 1842, p. 2.

151 Jenkins, M. (1980), p. 196.

152 *Manchester Times and Gazette*, Saturday, August 20, 1842, p. 2, col. 5.

153 *Halifax Guardian*, July 23 1842, p. 5.

154 This gave fuel to the Chartists' firmly held belief that the strike was orchestrated by the Anti-Corn Law League as a way towards tipping Government opinion in their favour. see Thompson, D. (1986), p. 283.

155 William Duffy, tailor, in O'Connor, F. (1843), p. 167.

156 In Thompson p. 292.

157 Crabtree, J. (1836), p. 400 and *Halifax Guardian*, June 25 1840, p. 6.

158 A fustian cutter by trade, Joseph Greenwood became a leading figure in the nineteenth century cooperative movement in Britain. In Hanson, T. W. (1920), p. 255.

159 Joseph Lawson, J. (1887), pp. 132-3.

160 Wilson, B. (1887), p. 4.

161 Joseph Greenwood, in Hanson, T. W. (1920), p. 256.

162 *Halifax Guardian*, Aug 20, 1842, p. 4.

163 Joseph Greenwood, in Hanson, T. W. (1920), p. 256.

164 HO 45/264-79.

165 *Halifax Guardian*, Aug 20, 1842, p. 4, cols. 2-3.

166 Wilson, B. (1887), p. 4.

167 Peel, F. (1880), pp. 338-9.

168 *Halifax Guardian*, Aug 20, 1842, p.4, col. 3.

169 HO 45/268 in Jenkins, M. (1980), pp. 194-5.

170 *Halifax Guardian*, Aug 20, 1842, p.4, col. 3.

171 Francis Grundy was related to John Hancock, American Declaration of Independence signatory. He was also a faithful friend to Branwell Brontë, brother of Charlotte and Emily, who was working at the Luddenden Foot railway station at this time. He describes Branwell Brontë as 'a man moving in a mist, who lost his way'. (Grundy, F. H. (1879), p. 92).

172 Grundy, F. H. (1879), pp. 99-100.

173 Grundy, F. H. (1879), p. 100.

174 HO 45/264-112. Magistrate George Pollard says this contingent was accompanied by four of the Police.

175 Grundy, F. H. (1879), p. 101.

176 Grundy, F. H. (1879), p. 102.

177 *Halifax Guardian*, Aug 20, 1842, p. 4 col. 4.

178 *Northern Star and Leeds General Advertiser*, Saturday, Aug 20, 1842.

179 Grundy, F. H. (1879), p. 103.

180 HO 45/264-113.

181 Wilson, B. (1887), p. 5 and HO 45/264-113.

182 Grundy, F. H. (1879), p. 103.

183 Grundy, F. H. (1879), p. 104.

184 *Leeds Mercury*, Aug 20, 1842.

185 WO 12/1004.

186 Wilson, B. (1887), p. 5.

187 WO 12/1005.

188 Grundy, F. H. (1879), p.104.

189 HO 45/264-112-14.

190 *Halifax Guardian*, Aug 20, 1842, p.4 col 4-5.

191 HO 45/264.

192 Grundy, F. H. (1879), pp. 104-5.

193 *Halifax Guardian*, Aug 20, 1842, p.4, col. 5; and HO 45/264-175.

194 *Halifax Guardian*, Aug 20, 1842 p. 4, col. 5.

195 *Northern Star*, Aug 20, 1842 p. 5, col.1.

196 *Halifax Guardian*, Aug 20, 1842, p. 4, col. 5.

197 Wilson, B. (1887), p. 5.

198 *Halifax Guardian*, Aug 20, 1842, p.4, col. 5.

199 *Halifax Guardian*, Aug 20, 1842, p. 5, col. 6.

200 Grundy, F. H. (1879), p. 103.

201 HO 45/264-173.

202 *Halifax Guardian*, Aug 20, 1842, p. 5 cols. 3 & 4.

203 *Halifax Guardian*, Aug 20, 1842, p. 6, col. 1.

204 *Halifax Guardian*, Aug 20, 1842, p. 5, col. 5.

205 HO 45/264-93.

206 HO 45/264 -171.

207 *Halifax Guardian*, Aug 20, 1841, p. 4, col. 5.

208 HO 45/264-175.

209 *Halifax Guardian*, Aug 20, 1842, p. 4, col. 6.

210 *Halifax Guardian*, Aug 20, 1842, p. 4, col. 1.

NOTES

211 See *Halifax Guardian*, Aug 20, 1842, p. 4, cols. 5-6.

212 *Halifax Guardian*, Aug 20, 1842, p. 6, col. 3.

213 *Halifax Guardian*, Aug 20, 1842, p. 6, cols. 3-4.

214 Oastler, R. (1842), p. 1.

215 Oastler, R. (1842), pp. 279-80.

216 *Halifax Guardian*, Aug 27, 1842, p. 5.

217 *Northern Star*, Aug 20, 1842, p. 8.

218 *Northern Star*, Aug 27, 1842, p. 8, col. 5.

219 *Halifax Guardian*, Aug 20, 1842, p. 4.

220 *Bradford Observer*, May 23, 1839, p. 4, col. 2.

221 Wilson, B. (1887), p. 6.

222 WO 12/1005; Jenkins, M. (1980), p. 221.

223 HO 40/59-187.

224 HO 45/264-285; and *Halifax Guardian*, Aug 27, 1842, p. 5.

225 *Walker's Directory* 1845, p. 39.

226 see Hamish Fraser, J. (1999), p. 22.

227 From the Committee Room, Wakefield, 25 Sept 1842, in the *Northern Star and Leeds General Advertiser*, Saturday, October 1, 1842.

228 Challinor, R. & B. Ripley (1968), pp. 7, 8.

229 W. P. Roberts was the nephew of the judge, Sir Nicholas Tyndal, who had presided over John Frost's trial.

230 *Edinburgh Review*, Vol LIX (1834) p. 349, in *Trade Unions in the Victorian Age,* (1973) Vol I.

231 See Washington, pp.81, 84.

232 *Northern Star*, May 11, 1843, p. 9.

233 O'Connnor, F (1843), pp. 353, 355.

234 *Leeds Mercury*, Oct 16, 1830, p. 4, col. 2.

235 *Halifax and Huddersfield Express*, March 12, 1831, pp. 1, 4.

236 Ranger, W. (1851), p. 106.

237 Crabtree, J. (1836), p. 346.

238 Ward, J. T. (1962), p. 50.

239 In Jowitt, J. A. (1976), p. 181.

240 In Wesley-Bready, J. (1926), p. 188.

241 *Northern Star and Leeds General Advertiser*, February 24, 1844.

242 Gammage, R. G. (1894), p. 55.

243 In Finn, M. C. (1993), p. 229.

244 Mulroy, J. J. (1948), p. 30.

245 Washington p. 97.

246 Gammage, R. G. (1894), pp. 14, 45.

NOTES

247 Hargreaves, J. A. (2006), p. 24. Kate Tiller in Epstein, p. 311 quotes a different number.

248 See Gammage, R. G. (1894), p. 316.

249 In Cole, G. D. H. (1941), p. 341.

250 Wilson, B. (1887), pp. 9-10.

251 *Northern Star and National Trades' Journal,* July 10, 1847.

252 *Halifax Guardian*, 31 July 1847, p. 7, col 1.

253 *The Northern Star*, March 25 1848 and *Bradford Observer*, April 13, 1848.

254 Wilson, B. (1887) pp. 10, 11.

255 Thompson, D. & E. P., (unpublished), p. 66.

256 *Halifax Guardian*, April 21, 1848, p. 8.

257 *Northern Star and National Trades' Journal*, June 10, 1848.

258 *Preston Guardian* in Hargreaves, J.A. (2006), p. 22.

259 Wilson, B. (1887), p. 12.

260 In Cole, G. D. H. (1941), pp. 345-6.

261 Cole, G. D. H. (1941), pp. 346-9.

262 *Halifax Guardian*, July 20, 1850, p. 6, col. 2.

263 Wilson, B. (1887), p. 16.

264 In Hargreaves, J. A. (2006), p. 25.

265 Lawson, J. (1887), p. 89.

266 Wilson, B. (1887), p. 22.

267 Wilson, B. (1887), pp. 22, 23.

268 *Halifax Courier*, Sept 6, 1884.

269 In Tiller, K. (1982), p. 335.

270 Tiller, K. (1982), pp. 334, 326-332.

271 *Bradford Observer*, 28 Feb 1861, p. 6.

272 *Halifax Guardian*, 16 March 1861, p. 5.

273 Thompson D. & E. P. (unpublished) pp. 8, 96.

274 *Halifax Courier*, 6 Sept 1884 p. 7.

275 Wilson, B. (1887), p. 34.

276 25 June 1850 'Don Pacifico' speech taken from Wikisource.

277 Tiller, K. (1982), p. 338 and Malcolm Bull's *Calderdale Companion*.

278 *Halifax Courier*, 6 Sept 1884, p. 7.

279 powerinthelandscape.co.uk website and Onslow Garnett, W. (1951).

280 See Best, G. (1971), pp. 137-9; and Challinor, R. & B. Ripley (1968), p. 49.

281 Wesley Bready, J. (1926), p. 26.

282 *First Report of the Children's Employment Commission (Mines) 1842*. p. 16.

283 *Northern Star and Leeds General Advertiser*, 31 Dec 1842, p. 7, co.l 2.

284 The Coal Mining History Resource Centre website is an invaluable source of mining

history, based on Ian Winstanley's research.

285 *Leeds Mercury*, 27 October 1870; p. 7, col. 1.

286 Challinor, R. & B. Ripley (1968), p. 64.

287 Stanley Road Hospital medical case book records C85/3/6/20/p333A-333B/1, held at Wakefield Archives.

288 Crichton Browne, J. (1871), p. iv.

INDEX

INDEX

INDEX

Ralph Anstis, Warren James and the Dean Forest Riots, *The Disturbances of 1831*
£14.00 • 242pp *paperback* • 191x235mm • ISBN 978-0-9564827-7-8

The full story of the riots in the Forest of Dean in 1831, and how they were suppressed, is told here for the first time.

The book also gives the background to the riots; it discusses the simple lives of the foresters before the arrival in Dean of the Industrial Revolution, and how they lived in the Forest, pasturing their animals there and using it as if it was their own. It also describes the ancient way the free miners used to mine their iron and coal and how they regulated their mining activities through their Mine Law Court.

It sets out the two main causes of the riots: the determination of the government to enclose large areas of the Forest for growing timber, thus restricting the foresters' access; and the influx of 'foreigners' eager to exploit not only the Forest's coal and iron resources but also the foresters themselves.

Dominating the story is the enigmatic character of Warren James, the self-educated free miner who led the foresters in their attempt to stave off their increasing poverty and unemployment, and to protect their traditional way life from the threats of advancing industrial change. The tragic account of his unfair trial, his transportation to a convict settlement in Van Diemen's Land (Tasmania), his reprieve for political reasons, and his death far from the Forest is set against the background of the sordid and heartless times in which he lived

John E. Archer, 'By a Flash and a Scare', *Arson, Animal Maiming, and Poaching in East Anglia 1815-1870*
£12.00 • 206pp *paperback* • 191x235mm • ISBN 978-0-9564827-1-6

'By a Flash and a Scare' illuminates the darker side of rural life in the nineteenth century. Flashpoints such as the Swing riots, Tolpuddle, and the New Poor Law riots have long attracted the attention of historians, but here John E. Archer focuses on the persistent war waged in the countryside during the 1800s, analysing the prevailing climate of unrest, discontent, and desperation.

Victor Bailey, Charles Booth's Policemen, *Crime, Police and Community in Jack-the-Ripper's London*
£17.00 • 162pp *paperback* • 2 *colour and 8 b/w images* • 140x216mm • ISBN 978-0-9564827-6-1

What explains the law-abidingness of late Victorian England? A number of modern historians contend that the answer lies with the effectiveness of policing, and with the imposition of a 'policeman-state' in Victorian and Edwardian England.

Exploiting the vast archive that Charles Booth amassed for his leviathan social investigation to explore the social order of London's East End, *Life and Labour of the People in London*, this volume takes issue with this answer.

The East End was notorious as a region of unalleviated poverty, crime and immorality, the district where the issue of large-scale Jewish immigration was first confronted, and where Jack-the-Ripper found his victims.

Victor Bailey reveals that historians have overestimated the extent to which policemen were able or willing to intervene in the daily behaviour of inhabitants to suppress law breaking. He shows that the commission and repression of crime were linked not only to the structures of law enforcement but also to levels of community solidarity, associational life, family integration, and parental authority.

Social order was a function less of policing than of a complex combination of informal family and community sanctions, the mixed welfare of charity and state support, the new board schools, slum clearance, and the negotiated justice of the magistrates' courts.

The conclusions should lead us to question the role of the state in the making of social order, and to reinstate the force of informal social sanctioning.

Victor Bailey, Order and Disorder in Modern Britain, *Essays on Riot, Crime, Policing and Punishment*
£15.00 • 214pp *paperback* • 5 *b/w images* • 191x235mm • ISBN 978-0-9570005-5-1

The pieces in this collection range from an account of the Skeleton Army riots against the Salvation Army in the early 1880s to the unsuccessful campaign to abolish the death penalty in the aftermath of the Second World War. They include essays on how the Home Office and Metropolitan Police responded to the unemployed riots in the West End of London in 1886 and the contest over the right to assemble in Trafalgar Square in 1887; on the complex relationship between the Salvation Army's social scheme and the early labour movement; on the changing meanings inscribed within the term "dangerous and criminal classes"; and on English penal culture from the Gladstone Committee's Report on Prisons (1895) to the Labour Research Department's Prison System Enquiry Committee's report, English Prisons Today (1922).

The essays in this volume, (first published between 1977 and 2000), are coherent expressions, if not of a single philosophy, at least of a recurrent theme. That theme is the relationship between order and disorder in England over the century from 1850. Despite the stress fractures caused by deepening industrialization, strengthening class mobilization, and cyclical economic dislocation, Britain was a relatively peaceable kingdom in these years. Who and what were responsible for the imposition of social order?

In these essays, the emphasis is less on coercive policing, less on the conditioning of the working poor by 'moral entrepreneurs' into a set of desirable behaviours — though these doubtless played their part — and much more on the role of informal and autonomous communal and class codes; on the social and moral differentiation between the 'respectable working class' and the 'residuum', a normative ditch working people helped to dig and guard; and on popular support for, or at least popular participation in, the formal mechanisms of law and punishment.

Bob Bushaway, By Rite, *Custom, Ceremony and Community in England 1700-1880*
£14.00 • 206pp *paperback* • 191x235mm • ISBN 978-0-9564827-6-1

Political philosophers (such as Gramsci) and social historians (such as E. P. Thompson) have suggested that rural customs and ceremonies have much more to them than the picturesqueness which has attracted traditional folklorists. They can be seen to have a purpose in the structures of rural society. But no historian has really pursued this idea for the English folk materials of the eighteenth and nineteenth centuries: the period from which most evidence survives.

Bringing together a wealth of research, this book explores the view that rural folk practices were a mechanism of social cohesion, and social disruption. Through them the interdependence of the rural working-class and the gentry was affirmed, and infringements of the rights of the poor resisted, sometimes aggressively.

Malcolm Chase, The People's Farm, *English Radical Agrarianism 1775-1840*
£12.00 • 212pp *paperback* • 152x229mm • ISBN 978-0-9564827-5-4

This book traces the development of agrarian ideas from the 1770s through to Chartism, and seeks to explain why, in an era of industrialization and urban growth, land remained one of the major issues in popular politics. Malcolm Chase considers the relationship between 'land consciousness' and early socialism; attempts to create alternative communities; and contemporary perceptions of nature and the environment. *The People's Farm* also provides the most extensive study to date of Thomas Spence, and his followers the Spenceans.

Malcolm Chase, Early Trade Unionism, *Fraternity, Skill and the Politics of Labour*
£14.00 • 248pp *paperback* • 191x235mm • ISBN 978-0-9570005-2-0

Once the heartland of British labour history, trade unionism has been marginalised in much recent scholarship. In a critical survey from the earliest times to the nineteenth century, this book argues for its reinstatement. Trade unionism is shown to be both intrinsically important and to provide a window onto the broader historical landscape; the evolution of trade union principles and practices is traced from the seventeenth century to mid-Victorian times. Underpinning this survey is an explanation of labour organisation that reaches back to the fourteenth century. Throughout, the emphasis is on trade union mentality and ideology, rather than on institutional history. There is a critical focus on the politics of gender, on the demarcation of skill and on the role of the state in labour issues. New insight is provided on the long-debated question of trade unions' contribution to social and political unrest from the era of the French Revolution through to Chartism.

Nigel Costley, West Country Rebels
£20.00 • 220pp *full colour illustrated paperback* • 216x216mm • ISBN 978-0-9570005-4-4

What comes to mind when you think of the West Country? Beautiful beaches and coastline perhaps, rich countryside and moorland, great historic sites such as Stonehenge or perhaps the grace of Regency Bath or the stunning design of Brunel's Clifton Suspension Bridge? You may think of the West Country as the peaceful, quiet corner of Britain where people visit for holidays or spend their retirement.

What may not spring to mind is the Western Rebellion against enclosures, the bloody battles for fair taxes, the Prayer Book Rebellion against an imposed English Bible, the turbulent years of the Civil War and the Monmouth Rebellion that ended with the ruthless revenge of Judge Jefferies. You may know little about the radical edge to the region's maritime past such as the naval mutinies, smuggling and struggle for safety.

The West Country was famous for its wool and cloth but the battles by textile workers is less well known. For generations communities around the South West organised and engaged in riot and uprising, for food, for access, for fair tax and to be heard in a society that denied most people the vote. Women were at the centre of many of these disputes and their battle with poverty and inequality is featured along with West Country women who challenged those that kept them out and held them back.

Trade unionism has many a West Country story to tell, from the Tolpuddle Martyrs in Dorset, the longest strike in Plymouth, the great china clay strike of 1913, 'Black Friday' in Bristol and the battle for rights at GCHQ in Cheltenham..

This book features these struggles along with the characters who defied convention and helped organise around dangerous ideas of freedom, equality and justice.

Barry Reay, The Last Rising of the Agricultural Labourers, *Rural Life and Protest in Nineteenth-Century England*
£12.00 • 192pp *paperback* • 191x235mm • ISBN 978-0-9564827-2-3

The Hernhill Rising of 1838 was the last battle fought on English soil, the last revolt against the New Poor Law, and England's last millenarian rising. The bloody 'Battle of Bosenden Wood', fought in a corner of rural Kent, was the culmination of a revolt led by the self-styled 'Sir William Courtenay'. It was also, despite the greater fame of the 1830 Swing Riots, the last rising of the agricultural labourers.

Barry Reay provides us with the first comprehensive and scholarly analysis of the abortive rising, its background, and its social context, based on intensive research, particularly in local archives. He presents a unique case-study of popular mobilization in nineteenth-century England, giving us a vivid portrait of the day-to-day existence of the farm labourer and the life of the hamlet. Dr. Reay explores the wider context of agrarian relations, rural reform, protest and control through the fascinating story of *The Last Rising of the Agricultural Labourers*.

Buchanan Sharp, In Contempt of All Authority, *Rural Artisans and Riot in the West of England, 1586-1660*
£12.00 • 204pp *paperback* • 191x235mm • ISBN 978-0-9564827-0-9

Two of the most common types of popular disorders in late Tudor and early Stuart England were the food riots and the anti-enclosure riots in royal forests. Of particular interest are the forest riots known collectively as the Western Rising of 1626-1632, and the lesser known disorders in the Western forests which took place during the English Civil War. The central aims of this volume are to establish the social status of the people who engaged in those riots and to determine the social and economic conditions which produced the disorders.

Dorothy Thompson, The Chartists, *Popular Politics in the Industrial Revolution*
£16.00 • 280pp *paperback* • 191x235mm • ISBN 978-0-9570005-3-7

The Chartists is a major contribution to our understanding not just of Chartism but of the whole experience of working-class people in mid-nineteenth century Britain. The book looks at who the Chartists were, what they hoped for from the political power they strove to gain, and why so many of them felt driven toward the use of physical force. It also studies the reactions of the middle and upper classes and the ways in which the two sides — radical and establishment — influenced each other's positions.

The book is a uniquely authoritative discussion of the questions that Chartism raises for the historian; and for the historian, student and general reader alike it provides a vivid insight into the lives of working people as they passed through the traumas of the industrial revolution.

E. P. Thompson, Whigs and Hunters, *The Origin of the Black Act*
£16.00 • 278pp *paperback* • 156x234mm • ISBN 978-0-9570005-2-0

With *Whigs and Hunters*, the author of *The Making of the English Working Class*, E. P. Thompson plunged into the murky waters of the early eighteenth century to chart the violently conflicting currents that boiled beneath the apparent calm of the time. The subject is the Black Act, a law of unprecedented savagery passed by Parliament in 1723 to deal with 'wicked and evil-disposed men going armed in disguise'. These men were pillaging the royal forest of deer, conducting a running battle against the forest officers with blackmail, threats and violence.

These 'Blacks', however, were men of some substance; their protest (for such it was) took issue with the equally wholsesale plunder of the forest by Whig nominees to the forest offices. And Robert Walpole, still consolidating his power, took an active part in the prosecution of the 'Blacks'. The episode is laden with political and social implications, affording us glimpses of considerable popular discontent, political chicanery, judicial inequity, corrupt ambition and crime.

David Walsh, Making Angels in Marble, *The Conservatives, the Early Industrial Working Class and Attempts at Political Incorporation*
£15.00 • 268pp *paperback* • 191x235mm • ISBN 978-0-9570005-0-6

In the first elections called under the terms of the 1832 Reform Act the Tory party appeared doomed. They had recorded their worst set of results in living memory and were organizationally in disarray as well, importantly, seemingly completely out of touch with the current political mood. During the intense pressure brought to bear by the supporters of political reform was the use of "pressure from without" and in this tactic the industrial working class were highly visible. Calls for political reform had been growing since the 1760s and given fresh impetus with the revolutions in America and France respectively. The old Tory party had been resistant to all but the most glaring corruption and abuse under the pre-Reform system, not least to the idea of extending the electoral franchise to the 'swineish multitude', as Edmund Burke notoriously described the working class. Yet within five years after the passing of reform the Conservatives — the natural heirs to the old Tory party — were attempting to politically incorporate sections of the working class into their ranks. This book examines how this process of making these 'Angels in Marble', to use Disraeli's phrase from a later era, took shape in the 1830s. It focuses on how a section of the industrial working class became the target of organizational inclusion into Peelite Conservatism and ultimately into the British party political system.

BREVIARY STUFF PUBLICATIONS
www.breviarystuff.org.uk

Roger Wells, Insurrection, *The British Experience 1795-1803*
£17.50 • 372pp *paperback* • 191x235mm • ISBN 978-0-9564827-3-0

A re-evaluation of the hoary problem of the question of revolution in Britain and Ireland during the allegedly dying years of the Age of Revolution.

On the 16 November 1802 a posse of Bow Street Runners raided the Oakley Arms, a working class pub in Lambeth, on the orders of the Home Office. Over thirty men were arrested, among them, and the only one of any social rank, Colonel Edward Marcus Despard. Despard and twelve of his associates were subsequently tried for high treason before a Special Commission, and Despard and six others were executed on 21 February 1803. It was alleged that they had planned to kill the King, seize London and overturn the government and constitution.

Until recently this event had been almost entirely neglected by historians, principally on the grounds that it was an *isolated* occurrence, the brainchild of a disgruntled and probably insane Irishman. The incident is relegated to a footnote in the relevant volume of the *Oxford History of England* and even then only in support of First Minister Addington's habitual 'calmness'.

Apologists speedily claimed that Despard was just another dupe of the supposedly notorious hoard of informers and *agents-provocateurs* employed by the younger Pitt and his supposed lackey, Addington, to support their outrageous assault on the constitutional freedoms and rights of Englishmen. One pamphlet attacking the revelations of the infamous Oliver the Spy, typically claimed that in 1817 Oliver was 'by no means a novice in matters of treason, but … was closely and deeply implicated in the mad schemes of Colonel Despard'. These views, that any insurrectionary activity manifested by Englishmen was either the product of insane individuals or the manipulations of secret-service agents, or both, rather than an indigenous phenomenon, were also adopted by Whig and Fabian historians.

The first coherent reappraisal of the Despard affair was provided by E. P. Thompson, in his magnificent work, *The Making of the English Working Class*. An integral part of Thompson's thesis hinges on his analysis of what happened to one seminal political development in the 1790s, namely the first primarily English working-class movement for democracy. E. P. Thompson's claim that determined physical force revolutionary groupings originated after the suppression of the Popular Democratic Movement in 1795 has been seriously challenged by conventional British historians. This book offers a reinterpretation of Thompson's evidence, through a detailed overall study of post-1795 British politics. It throws new light on the organisation of government intelligence sources, Pitt's repressive policies and machinery, and oscillating popular responses; all developments, including recrudescences of the open Democratic Movement, and notably the emergence of insurrectionary conspiracies, are firmly related to both events in the critical Irish theatre, and the course of the war against France.

Roger Wells, Wretched Faces, *Famine in Wartime England 1793-1801*
£18.00 • 412pp *paperback* • 191x235mm • ISBN 978-0-9564827-4-7

This book reverts Malthus in a thoroughly English context. It proves that famine could, and *did*, occur in England during the classic period of the Industrial Revolution. The key economic determinant proved to be the ideologically-inspired war, orchestrated by the Prime Minister, the younger Pitt, against the French and their attempted export of revolutionary principles at bayonet point, to the rest of Europe. This international context, in part, conditioned the recurrent development of famine conditions in England in 1794-6 and again in 1799-1801. Here the multiple ramifications of famine in this country, as it lurched from crisis to crisis in wartime, are explored in considerable depth. These were repeated crises of capitalism, juxtaposed with the autocratic and aristocratic state's total commitment to war, which contrived to challenge not just the commitment to war, but both the equilibrium and the survival of the state itself. 'WANT' stalked the land; intense rioting periodically erupted; radical politicisation, notably of unenfranchised working people, proceeded apace, in part stimulated by the catastrophic events projected on the world stage by the process of the French Revolution. The book finally explains how such an oligarchic, unrepresentative government managed through determined economic interventionism, manipulation of the unique English social security system, and final resort to army rule, to preserve itself and the political structure during a key epoch within the Age of Revolutions.

Lightning Source UK Ltd.
Milton Keynes UK
UKHW011821170322
400229UK00002B/23